THE MAIDU INDIAN
MYTHS AND STORIES
OF HANC´IBYJIM

A California Legacy Book

Santa Clara University and Heyday Books are pleased to publish the California Legacy series, vibrant and relevant writings drawn from California's past and present.

Santa Clara University—founded in 1851 on the site of the eighth of California's original twenty-one missions—is the oldest institution of higher learning in the state. A Jesuit institution, it is particularly aware of its contribution to California's cultural heritage and its responsibility to preserve and celebrate that heritage.

Heyday Books, founded in 1974, specializes in critically acclaimed books on California literature, history, natural history, and ethnic studies.

Books in the California Legacy series appear as anthologies, single author collections, reprints of important books, and original works. Taken together, these volumes bring readers a new perspective on California's cultural life, a perspective that honors diversity and finds great pleasure in the eloquence of human expression.

Series editor: Terry Beers
Publisher: Malcolm Margolin
Advisory committee: Stephen Becker, William Deverell, Charles Faulhaber, David Fine, Steven Gilbar, Ron Hansen, Gerald Haslam, Robert Hass, Jack Hicks, Timothy Hodson, James Houston, Jeanne Wakatsuki Houston, Maxine Hong Kingston, Frank LaPena, Ursula K. Le Guin, Jeff Lustig, Tillie Olsen, Ishmael Reed, Alan Rosenus, Robert Senkewicz, Gary Snyder, Kevin Starr, Richard Walker, Alice Waters, Jennifer Watts, Al Young.

Thanks to the English Department at Santa Clara University and to Regis McKenna for their support of the California Legacy series.

For a complete list of California Legacy titles, please visit
www.californialegacy.org.

CALIFORNIA
LEGACY

THE MAIDU INDIAN MYTHS AND STORIES OF HANC'IBYJIM

Edited and translated by
William Shipley

Foreword by Gary Snyder

SANTA CLARA UNIVERSITY, SANTA CLARA, CALIFORNIA
HEYDAY BOOKS, BERKELEY, CALIFORNIA

Heyday Books, founded in 1974, works to deepen people's understanding and appreciation of the cultural, artistic, historic, and natural resources of California and the American West. It operates under a 501(c)(3) nonprofit educational organization (Heyday Institute) and, in addition to publishing books, sponsors a wide range of programs, outreach, and events.

To help support Heyday or to learn more about us, visit our website at www.heydaybooks.com, or write to us at P.O. Box 9145, Berkeley, CA 94709.

ISBN: 0-930588-52-5
Library of Congress Card Catalog Number: 91-070319

Cover illustration by Harry Fonseca
Interior design by Rick Heide

Orders, inquiries, and correspondence should be addressed to:
Heyday Books
P. O. Box 9145, Berkeley, CA 94709
(510) 549-3564, Fax (510) 549-1889
www.heydaybooks.com

Printed in the United States of America

10 9 8 7 6 5 4 3

Contents

Foreword   vii

Introduction   1

The Maidu People   5

In the Beginning of the World   17

Tales of Old Man Coyote   65

Tales of Other Beings   117

Appendix   177

Dedication

In memory of my Maidu teacher,
Maym Hannah Benner Gallagher.
A very great lady.

Foreword

How, I wonder—how, I wonder—
in what place, I wonder—
where, I wonder—
in what sort of place might we two see a bit of land?

There might be a place of land. It would have a snow mountain to the north, a blue-grey expanse to the east, ridges and canyons to the south, and a broad valley to the west that leads to further mountains and finally to the edge of the world. This land might have great meadows, beautiful parklands, bare granite ridges, and splendid fast streams and rivers. It might be someone's home.

It *was* someone's home, for tens of thousands of years. They were *maydy,* "creatures," "beings" of thousands of sorts, which included *wonom maydy,* "human creatures." These "maidu," human beings of the running ridges, deeply forested canyons, and mountain meadow lands of the northern California Sierra, tell a wonderful set of tales about their fellow-creatures and their place. They tell it from the beginning.

This collection opens with an outstanding creation myth. It was told to turn-of-the-century anthropologist Roland Dixon by a renowned storyteller named Hánc'ibyjim, "Tom Young." His language was Northeastern Maidu. In the early fifties a young linguistic anthropologist named William Shipley took up Maidu studies with an elderly woman named Diculto, Lena Thomas Benner. Her daughter Maym Benner Gallagher and Shipley went over Dixon's texts again, to come up with what is surely one of the richest sets of old-time Turtle Island texts available.

At the beginning it seems there were two sacred characters running around together, arguing, planning, constructing, taking apart, disagreeing, and making a universe. *K'ódojape* and *Wépam wájsy,* Earthmaker and Coyote Old Man, they quarrel like lovers—but there's a little bit more to it than just *kvetching* between friends.

*Wanting a bit of land
imagining it to be somewhere
singing it into being*

And the two find a little bit of land floating, stretch it, form it, visualizing what it could become. Then these two sacred goofy buddies come up with the idea of "many creatures" and specific habitat for each. They pick a "little creature" out of somewhere, and make a plan that when this little guy gets big enough, the he's and she's will have names for things and they'll have a "country." These are the humans.

And there are songs. Earthmaker gives them to all beings—

*There will be songs—
there will always be songs,
and all of you will have them.*

Coyote is no stranger, now, to the twentieth century Euroamerican imagination. There are several widely differing interpretations of what he might be. He is seen as a sort of rock musician shaman, or as a culture-hero/trickster who holds contradictory powers and plays a role that is sometimes creative and sometimes destructive, or an archetype of the immature unsocialized ego, or a perennial witty amoral survivor; sometimes he is even the outright principle of evil, the devil.

Coyote is a big presence in this collection, in every sense, and it is worth looking closely at the role he plays in "creating/ defining" the present world. It will not ruin the story that lies ahead to say a little about it. These two characters that are forming (or defining) the world are not, I am sure, representing good and evil principles slugging it out inconclusively. They step together through a dialectic, a dialog, of ideal and real, with a sinewy final resolution that takes the world as it is. Even as Earthmaker hopes for a universe without pain and death, Coyote argues for impermanence, for things as they *are*. As Earthmaker fantasizes a world in which unmarried girls remain virgins and married couples remain celibate, Coyote calls for tickling, lovemaking, and whispering to each other. Earthmaker has a plan for immortality, Coyote insists that there be death. Coyote wins out, and Earthmaker wanders off, to remain in isolation somewhere "down below." Coyote goes on to finish defining the world which is our present reality.

Earthmaker proposes an ideal, Coyote presents the phenomenal. For a spell Earthmaker and Coyote shape the world almost as partners. And finally, Coyote attends to a world totally phenomenal, but one that is fluid, shape-shifting, role-playing, painful and dirty, but also cheerfully transcended. If Coyote stands up for *samsara,* the actuality of birth-and-death, it is part of the ultimate paradox that he cannot be killed. He always pulls his scattered conditional self together again, and goes trotting on. In the ongoing tales of Old Man Coyote, we see what could be called "jokes of *samsara*" played out: outrageous, offensive, and ultimately liberating—into rueful acceptance, courage, and humor.

There are tales of other beings too. What realities are echoed! When the Cottontail boys tease Woodrat, "Old Woodrat makes me puke! Shitting on his grandmother's blankets—stinking everything up—pissing on everything—yucky old Woodrat! Makes his whole house stink!" we are getting an angle on the several-millenia-old woodrat middens found preserved in caves or overhangs in the Great Basin, containing solidified urine and antique fecal pellets at the ancient twig bottoms. These are useful for radiocarbon dating, and pushing the dating-scale farther back.

Perhaps we have heard too much of Coyote. There are would-be coyotes hanging out all over the western United States. He has totally overshadowed the other figures of western North American oral literature. This is partly because he has not been kept "secret." There are narratives that were never trapped in writing and are not told to outsiders that might balance this emphasis. The story of Mountain Lion and his long search for his lost children is of a different realm, unfolding in real time. Moon is a compulsive child-kidnapper and it takes the persistent old woman Frog to set him straight (even though she can't quite manage to swallow him). Also there are dramatic moments in these tales as old as any telling, that make them part of that truly ancient international lore that underlies the later "world classics." We are drawn into the aura of the giant serpent who would love a human girl, raising his great head and staring intently in her eyes, night after night. We have known the teenage girls who danced and talked and dreamed of having stars for lovers, and then got them and *that* was trouble. We gingerly feel our way into

> *Moon was living with his sister.*
> *Their house was coated with ice.*

The world of Native American myths and stories is not exactly pleasant. Captured wives, stolen children, hard-dealt death. Some would say that we should be grateful to Coyote for making things challenging. Coyotes are still around, the stories are still vivid, and the People are still here, too. The relatives of Hánc'ibyjim and Maym Gallagher are alive and well, keeping their culture alive, and playing a strong role in the future of their bioregion.

These myths and stories are unsweetened, unsentimental, and irreducible. They are a profound little chunk of world literature, and they are the first, but not the last, stories to be told of where we are learning to live: the little watershed of northern California, the big watershed of the planet.

Gary Snyder
Kitkitdizze, San Juan Ridge
Shasta Bioregion

Introduction

Introduction

During the Christmas holidays of 1954, I drove up into the Northern Sierra Nevada of California in search of a fluent speaker of the Maidu language, one of more than eighty languages (no one knows exactly how many there were) which were spoken in that part of North America which we now call California. I was a graduate student at the University of California at Berkeley, in the field of linguistics. My plan was to learn Maidu and to write, as a Ph.D. dissertation, a description of its grammar. I succeeded in doing that, and, in the process, I had one of the richest and most valuable experiences of my life. I had the incredible good fortune to get acquainted with the family of Lena Thomas Benner. Mrs. Benner, then in her nineties, could remember the times when the Maidu were living more or less in their traditional way. She married a white man, Thaddeus Benner, and had many descendants, some of whom I got to know and claim as friends.

Paramount among these was one of her daughters, Maym Benner Gallagher, a woman of remarkable abilities, who was perfectly bilingual in Maidu and English and who became my teacher and mentor. She, too, had married a white man and, though herself childless, had raised several nieces and nephews—in fact, she continued taking in children from her extended family for the rest of her life.

Maym had a high school education. Bright and articulate, with a rollicking sense of humor, she was equipped by temperament and experience to bring together and control the themes of both Maidu and Euroamerican culture. My personal bond with her was warm, affectionate and, for me at least, immensely rewarding. I have never had a better or more understanding friend. She made learning the Maidu language an intense and delicious experience.

In 1902 and 1903, the American Museum of Natural History in New York sent a group of scientists and scholars to California to study, among other things, the Native American cultures and languages. This enterprise, known as the Huntington Expedition, had as one of its members a Harvard scholar named Roland B. Dixon who made a study of the Maidu language, including the collecting and transcribing of a large number of myths and stories. Several years later, in 1912, these were published in Maidu, with English translations. In his introduction to that work, Dixon says: "All of the texts were secured at Genesee, Plumas County, California from Tom Young, a half Maidu, half Atsugewi man, who, although only about thirty years of age, possessed an extensive knowledge of the myths of the Maidu of this region."

I took this book of Dixon's with me to Maym in 1956, at the beginning of my second summer of work with her. She had not known about the book, but she knew very well who Tom Young had been—the last great Maidu storyteller. His real Indian name, I found out, had been Hánc'ibyjim. We were both fascinated by the stories recorded in the book but, for some reason which I can not now recall, we only worked together to reconstitute the trickster cycle—the part which in the present volume is called *Tales of Old Man Coyote*. Time passed, other matters intervened. I only saw Maym for short visits; then, many years later, she died.

Though I never forgot the Dixon recordings, I just assumed, without really checking, that the language was too difficult, that I could never work it out alone. It was certainly true that Hánc'ibyjim's Maidu was much more elaborate in vocabulary and syntax than the Maidu spoken by my friends in the '50s. But, one day, about ten years ago, I took the book off the shelf and set my hand to reconstituting the beginning of the Creation Myth. To my considerable surprise, I was able to infer what Hánc'ibyjim had really said with an amazing amount of confidence—though certainly not at lightning speed. Furthermore, it dawned on me that the texts are more than just a trove for linguists, that the myths are possessed of great style and beauty, that they are real works of oral literary art, or perhaps it would be more perceptive to say that they are works of dramatic art—in Euroamerican terms, a kind of melding of poetry and theater. In my translations, I have constantly been at pains to maintain this oral, theatrical quality of the originals.

Though the evidence is fragmentary, the stories lead one to some perception of the old original Maidu world-view, now for so long lost in time. Take, for example, the word 'Maidu' itself. It is an Anglicized version of *máydy,* which, on the face of it, is the word for 'person' or 'man' or, if plurality is in the context, 'people.' And that's the way it is used among twentieth century Maidu speakers (perhaps I should say "was" since I know of only a very few very old people who still have any competence with the language). But the stories have a much larger semantic domain for *máydy*! At the very beginning of the Creation Myth, for example, there is a sentence which means, in part: "There were no different kinds of *máydy* flying about." Dixon translates this as: "No persons of any kind flew about." But that just doesn't make sense. It turns out that this example, along with many others, points to a meaning for *máydy* like 'creature' or 'being.' That this is the right way to look at it is reinforced by the persistent use of a phrase *wónom máydy* whenever human beings are to be specified in contrast with other creatures. Thus it would seem that, to the Maidu, human beings were just a subset of beings, implying a world-view wildly at variance with traditional Judeo-Christian culture but singularly consonant with post-Darwinian humanism.

Many Euroamericans, so far as I can tell, still tend to think of Native Americans either as hopelessly childlike ex-savages or as incredibly noble and wise iconic dehumanized super-persons. What I would most hope from this book is that it bring home to its readers at least the sense of the Maidu as real people—interesting, vital, sexy, full of fantasies and dreams—in short, like people everywhere, as soon as you get a chance to know them.

The Maidu
People

The Maidu People

For thousands of years, before the Europeans even knew of their existence, the American continents were home to several million people. These people, with a bewildering variety of languages, customs and oral traditions, lived on the land from time immemorial. In North America itself, one of the oldest areas of settlement was that land which we now call Central and Northern California. There, in a condition of elegant social equipoise, lived many small groups of people, speaking many different languages. Though all of these groups hunted, fished and gathered food in similar ways, their oral literary traditions were often dramatically distinctive.

The myths and tales in this book are those of the Maidu, whose original homeland was in California, at the northern end of the Sierra Nevada, just east and south of Mount Lassen—the West Mountain which turns up in several of the stories. The Maidu people still live there today, carrying on many of their timeless traditions and stoutly maintaining their identity. Except for a few elderly persons, no one now speaks the old language and many of the old customs are lost. Much still remains, however—notably a reverence for the old times and for their ancestors. The women still make beautiful baskets. The traditional Bear Dance is still held in late June every year. There are still Big Times with acorn bread and other great things to eat. On festive occasions, people still play the Grass Game all through the day and far into the night.

In pre-conquest times, the Maidu lived along the margins of high mountain meadows, lush and well-watered in spring and early summer, drier in late summer and autumn, and buried, through the winter, in a deep covering of snow. These meadows were interludes in a boundless virgin forest of pine, fir, cedar and deciduous growth, including the oak trees which provided their staple food. The glory and beauty of this lofty, roadless landscape can today only be appreciated by an act of imagination. The forest was not trackless—the trails of humans and animals went to wherever there was reason to go. The people burned out the underbrush, too, every year, opening vistas through the aisles of the forest, making it easier to move about and giving the forests what later explorers called a 'park-like' appearance.

The largest social units were small villages near to each other, in clusters, just across the meadow or a few yards upstream. In each village, there was a man who had been selected by the elders for his astuteness and generosity as the informal leader and arbiter of village affairs. He organized all the communal events—deer drives, acorn harvesting, feasts, Big Times, the building of a new ceremonial lodge, and so on. This man was called the *yopónim.*

The spiritual leaders were called *yomím máydym.* Both men and women could be *yomím,* though there was a tendency for women to be more knowledgeable about the use of herbal remedies, while the men were more inclined to make use of magic power over the realm of good and evil spirits. The commonest practical use made of these various powers was for the treatment of illnesses and ailments. The idea of accumulating and controlling power was at the heart of the matter. The *yomím* had the power to invoke and direct entities in the spirit world, not only for the purpose of curing illness but also for influencing human affairs in other ways— casting spells for success in hunting, in love, in gambling. Anyone who had the call could aspire to become a successful *yomím.* The child, especially the son, of a *yomím* was expected to seek power and to become a *yomím* himself. Dan Williams, a *yomím* who was still alive in the 1950s, gave me an account of how, under the tutelage of his father (who was also a *yomím*), he received his power. The following is a translation:

> We were there, at Tobacco Dwelling Mountain Pool. My father, now dead, who was standing behind me, said: "You must always believe in yourself. I have brought you around to this place so that you will dive into the pool." So I dived in, then, down from a rock out in the middle of the pool. The water seemed to swirl and bubble, like this . . . [gesturing with his hands]. . . . When I dived deeper, leafy foliage seemed to hit me in the eyes, like this, though it was far off. I came up to the surface. Then my father said: "Do that again and make a grab when you are under the water. Perhaps you will grab

something, perhaps you won't but, if you do, hang onto it. If all goes well, a charm will be given to you. If you just make a grab in the water, you may take hold of something which, perhaps, is drifting around in the pool." I dived again, I brought up that charm, I took hold of a charmstone. And when I looked down at it in my hand, my father said: "Good! You did well. A gambling charm has been given you." Then I swam back to shore. My father said: "You will always fare well, sitting down to the Grass Game. You will thrust the bones secretly into the grass with great success. Good has been given you on this trial for power, this entering of the pool. Gambling will go well for you, the charm has been given you, you will fare well. You will surpass me!" Thus my father spoke to me at the place where I came out on the bank.

This account of Dan Williams' boyhood experience represents only the beginning of his quest for power. The validation of a true *yomím* was a long and complex process. It involved first the acquisition of spirit helpers and masters through dreams and visions; then a demonstration, during winter seances in the ceremonial lodge, that one could control these spirits and successfully invoke their help in curing illness and casting spells.

In a ceremony of curing, the ailing person was laid on a mat in the ceremonial lodge. The *yomím* entered, dressed only in an otterskin headband or, if the case was particularly serious, in a *pálak'am* or headstall made of yellowhammer feathers. He had with him his cocoon rattles and a birdbone whistle. He began to sing, quietly at first, then with ever-increasing fervor, shaking and banging the rattles against the spirit-post and alternating his singing with increasingly intense and rhythmic birdbone whistling. This singing, rattling and whistling was by way of an invocation—a marshalling of his personal spirit guides and helpers whose arrival and participation would provide the power to find the *ítum*—the object or creature which had been 'shot' into the patient and was causing the sickness.

At the climax of the curing ceremony, the *yomím*, with more or less of a struggle, sucked out the *ítum* from the appropriate place on the patient's body and showed it to the patient and to the other people who were there. The *ítum* might be a tiny lizard, an insect, a pebble, a little frog—whatever it was, if it was removed skillfully and in time, the ailing person would get well.

In one of Coyote's adventures, he parodies the sacred mystery of the curing ceremony simply to satisfy his own lust:

> The old woman's daughter was in the hut.
> Coyote scooted along on his butt into the hut
> and sat down beside her.
> He started singing.
> "When a spirit speaks to me,
> it speaks like this:
> 'Being loath to do battle,
> I have always talked through you.
> I am the one who raps the spirit-post.
> If everyone closes up the house
> and makes it tight and strong,
> then I will speak through the *yomím.*
> If the people will crawl outside
> then I, myself, the spirit,
> will speak through the *yomím.*' "
>
> So the old woman crawled out,
> sealed up the hut and stayed outside.
>
> Meanwhile, Coyote was singing.
> It sounded loud and fast.
>
> The old woman said:
> "Now he must be curing her!
> He's fetching up a spirit of the dead with his doctoring!"
>
> There was a scary sound of heavy breathing.
> The old woman peeked through a cranny
> and saw that Coyote was lying on top of the girl,
> going at it hard and strong.

In each village cluster, there was a large communal earth lodge or *k'umúm,* the place where much of the ceremonial life of the people went on. These lodges were made by digging a circular pit about a yard deep and thirty feet or so in diameter. A triangular set of stout vertical posts was set up in the middle,

and the sides of the pit were lined with large pieces of bark
or split wood. Logs were laid around the circumference to
which the lower ends of the main rafters—usually eight—were
secured. The tops of the rafters were lashed to a triangular
assembly on top of the three center-posts. Smaller cross-poles
were laid over the rafters; over these poles were spread bark,
branches, pine needles and, finally, a layer of earth several
inches thick. A smokehole was left in the very center of the
lodge roof, directly over the triangular space formed by the
three center-posts. This smokehole was the main entrance to
the lodge—the one used by all the adults, who got into the
lodge by climbing down a steep interior notched ladder. A
very much smaller opening sloped up from the bottom of the
pit to ground level. This served as a draft for the fire and as
the entrance used by children and dogs. The center-post farthest
from this draft opening was the *sudók'om* or main spirit-post,
the sacred center of the lodge. The fireplace—a round hearth
of stones—was in front of this spirit-post, directly under the
smokehole.

The other permanent houses in the village were similar in
form to the ceremonial lodge, but smaller. In these, families
or groups of families lived. A door made of deerskin could
be used to cover the smokeholes on these houses, thus neatly
converting them into sweatlodges. The only other house types
were simple conical bark huts, built for a season and used
as menstrual huts or for casual summer living.

The women wore a kind of fore-and-aft apron made by tying
a stout cord around the waist to which was attached, in front
and back, bundles of softened maple or willow bark or, more
often, strips of buckskin decorated with deer hoofs or pine-
nuts. In good weather, the men and children wore nothing at
all except when they bedecked themselves on ceremonial
and festive occasions. Here, again, we must try to break free
of our own biases. Nakedness is a state of mind, an artifact
of our cultural tradition. It is vital to understand that the
Maidu did not 'run around naked.' Decorum took other
forms—no wise person, for example, would utter the name
of someone recently dead until after the yearly mourning
ceremony, nor would a woman, while menstruating, fail to

use a stick instead of her fingernails to scratch her head. Above all, a mother-in-law would go to great lengths to avoid any encounter with her son-in-law. In case of an accidental meeting, she would cover her head and make a low keening noise to warn him of her presence so that he might quickly and silently get away.

In winter, out of doors, the Maidu wore moccasins with leggings, stuffed with dry grass for warmth, and wrapped themselves in the skins of deer or mountain lions with the fur side in. Everyone's hair grew long and hung freely, though both men and women at times wore netted caps.

Hunting—with bows and arrows, spears, nets and snares—was done exclusively by the men. Edible game abounded; brown bears, elk, mountain lions, deer, mountain sheep, rabbits, raccoons and many other small animals and birds were eaten—virtually all creatures, in fact, except for grizzly bears, wolves, coyotes and dogs.

Most of the vegetable food was harvested by the women, though acorns were communally gathered. The men and big boys climbed the oak trees and knocked the acorns down, while the women and children picked them up off the ground. But the women alone did all of the elaborate preparation of the acorns: shelling, grinding, leaching, storing, cooking. And the women did all of the rest of the food preparation as well.

A brilliant tradition, unique to Native California, is the art of basketmaking which, with its wonderful combination of utility and beauty of conception, is probably unsurpassed anywhere in the world. This art and the complex skills and knowledge which make it possible are still carried on today among Maidu women—the gathering and preparation of willow stems, redbud, hazel, maidenhair fern and many other plants, the various techniques involved with weaving all the different shapes and sizes of baskets and with producing all their striking and traditional designs.

Making baskets remains, as it has always been, one of the great traditional activities of Maidu life. In the story of Moon and Frog Old Woman, Moon exploits Frog Old Woman's passion for her basketmaking art—for her willingness to be sidetracked even when her grandson has been kidnapped. As she pursues him, he delays her:

> Now, when Moon had run a little way along,
> by magic, he thought into being a stand of willows—
> a stand of willows, wonderful to see!
> And then, again, when he had come along a little further,
> he thought another stand of willows into being.
> And then he hastened on.
>
> The old woman, coming along behind,
> ran up to the stand of willows,
> still holding bunchgrass in her mouth.
> When she saw the willows, she said:
> "Well!
> I have never seen anything so big and wonderful!"
> And she stopped in her tracks and gathered some.

Festivities and Big Times were frequent. In the blossom time of early spring, when the dogwood and the first buttercups were blooming and the wormwood was in green leaf, then the women prepared lots of food—game and fish, acorn bread and soup—and the men got out their feather finery, their eagle-feather bustles and their yellowhammer-feather head-stalls. For several days, rubbed with wormwood leaves for the fragrance, bedecked with garlands of flowers and foliage, the people sang and danced, rejoicing in the return of clement weather. And, on the last day, they all ran down to the river and threw their garlands in, imploring the rattlesnakes to stay away. "Snake, snake, don't bite us!" they shouted. "Snake, look away into some other land! Just as these flowers float away from us down the river, you, snake, go away from us through all the summer and fall!" Then everyone would run back up and feast on all the great food the women had made ready.

In summer came the mysterious *yúkbom* or Bear Dance when important men, dressed in bearskins, imitated the lumbering movements of the bear. Since spirits of dead *yomím* were often reincarnated as bears, a kind of ominous spirituality infused this ceremony. Also in summer came the *jýpym solím* or girls' puberty ceremony, honoring all the girls who had started to menstruate during the year preceding.

Along with these more formal ceremonies, there were many Big Times when People got together for singing, dancing, gambling and feasting. When a *yopónim* wanted to invite people from the villages roundabout, he decided on how many days it would be until the good time was to be held. Then he took buckskin strings called *walásim*, tied a knot for each intervening day, and sent boys out in all directions, each with a string for one of the invited villages. Every day from then on, one knot was untied or cut away on every one of the strings. Thus, all of the invited guests knew when to arrive, and everyone got there on the same day.

On these festive occasions, the central pastime was the *sop'óm helám* or Grass Game, which remains to this day one of the centerpieces of traditional Maidu social life. It is played for the highest stakes—in former times, great quantities of personal possessions changed hands: beads, tools, regalia, baskets. Nowadays, the game is played for money. Single games sometimes go on for many days.

Four small cylinders of mountain lion bone, deer bone or wood are used, two or three inches long. There are two pairs of these bones; one of each pair is plain, while the other has a dark band around the middle. Counting sticks are also used, variable in number depending on how long the game is to go on.

The teams sit facing each other, usually with the fire between them. In front of them is a pile of dry grass in which the bones may be wrapped from time to time; hence the name of the game. The counting sticks are evenly divided between the two teams. By pre-arrangement, one team has the bones first, one pair in the hands of each of two players. While their teammates sing a gambling song, these two players pass the banded and unbanded bones from hand to hand, in front of and behind themselves and in the pile of grass. The opposing team, meanwhile, watches closely and, when the players with the bones cross their arms indicating that they are ready for the guessing to begin, one member of the opposing team makes a guess as to where the four bones are. With the players sitting side by side, there are four possibilities: banded bones in the left hands, banded bones in the right hands, banded bones in the middle, and banded bones on the outside. The guesser may try for either the banded or the unbanded bones. The two players holding the bones then open their hands and show where the bones actually are. If the guess was entirely wrong, the guessers pass across two counting sticks; if they get one pair right, they hand over one counting stick and get possession of that pair of bones; if they guess entirely right they get both pair of bones and, loudly singing a new gambling song, get to hide them in turn. The game goes on until one side has all the counting sticks.

Richard Smith, who, as a young student, attended the Bear Dance in Susanville in the early '60s, vividly described the experience in his journal:

> I watched the grass game played by Maidu vs. Paiute some-times—Paiute vs. Paiute, I think, a couple of times. I still don't understand the mechanics of the game completely, but everyone else bets on a team to win. Two lined teams, facing each other squarely. Songs and rhythm and chatter and signs and 'poker faces' (grass game faces), while 2 pairs of bones are shuffled around in the hands with flourishing gestures. I was thinking of the fantastic interplay—rhythm in sight and hearing and song; repetitious; ritual movements, some of them; diversionary and enjoyable chatter and signs; the always good humor, even when a disagreement arose; the laughter, the bystanders chatting back and forth; the tremendous con-centration and attention.
>
> The guessing side's watching was the most fascinating to me. Sometimes direct stares, glances, but usually moving, quick looks. The guess is made with following movements, and the answer is sometimes immediate, sometimes several minutes later. The bones and the sticks are tossed or thrown or pushed, usually with flourishes too.
>
> The responsibility to guess well is quite heavy, as is the responsibility to bluff well. I think there is a small amount of (here I run into trouble because we don't have a word that doesn't prejudge it) behind-the-scenes or undercover switch-ing, etc., because several times new bones were brought in, bigger and more difficult to switch.
>
> The men talk disdainfully of play against women, but the women hold their own and add, I think, a wonderful sense of happy enjoyment to the whole thing.

It is essential, when we talk of the Maidu world, not to fall victim to idyllic and romantic notions—those very notions which cause us to dehumanize Native Americans, to turn them into icons stuck in a kind of diorama of some Golden Age. Life, for the Maidu, was well supplied with pitfalls and troubles—the vicissitudes of getting born and living with constant vulnerability to the vagaries of nature—of weather, of accidents, of infection, the sheer terror which must often have come from the dark forests of the night. Perhaps the most important thing for us is to realize that countless generations really did live and die on this land and that they left behind, in these stories, an invaluable record for their own descendants as well as a fragment of their heritage for the enrichment of the human experience everywhere.

In the
Beginning of
the World

I. The Creation

And Earthmaker, they say,
when this world was covered with water,
floated and looked about him.

As he floated and looked about,
he did not see anywhere, indeed,
even a tiny bit of land.

No various creatures of any kind—
none at all were flying about.

And thus he travelled over this world,
over the engulfed land.

It seemed transparent,
like the land in the Meadows of Heaven.

And he felt sad, they say.
"How, I wonder—how, I wonder—
in what place, I wonder—
where, I wonder—
in what sort of place might we two see a bit of land?"

This is what he asked.

"Well, you are very powerful
to have thought this world into being!
Imagine where in this world
some land might be, then,
and when you have done so,
let us two float to that place.
If, in this world, you keep floating and looking around you,
floating and looking around you,
hungering, but indeed eating nothing,
you will die of hunger, I fear,"
said the other.

Then Earthmaker pondered.
"I shall not starve," he said.
"There's nothing I don't know.
The world is very big, it is true.
If, somewhere or other, I should see a bit of earth,
then I shall make something good of it."

Thereupon, he sang.

"Where are you, little bit of earth?"
He said it, singing.
He kept singing and singing.

"Enough," he said.
He stopped singing.

Coyote said:
"Indeed, there are not many songs that I don't know."
And then, after that, *he* sang,
kept on singing and singing.

"Where is there land?" he asked.
He sang and sang.

"Enough! I'm tired," he said.
"*You* try again!"

And then, they say, Earthmaker sang.
"Where are you, my great mountain ranges?
O, mountains of my world, where are you?"

Then, "Enough!" he said.
"See what *you* can do."

Coyote tried. He kept on singing.
"If, indeed, we two shall see nothing at all,
travelling about the world,
then, perhaps,
there may be no misty mountain ranges there!"

Earthmaker said:
"If I could but see a little bit of land
I might do something very good with it."

Floating along, then,
they saw something like a bird's nest.
Earthmaker said:
"It really is small.
It would be good if it were a little bigger,
but it is really small.
I wonder how I might stretch it apart a little.
What would be good to do?
In what way can I make it a little bigger?"

As he talked, he transformed it.

He stretched it out to where the day breaks;
he stretched it out to the south;
he stretched it out to the place where the sun goes down;
he stretched it out to the North Country;
he stretched it out to the rim of the world;
he stretched it out!

When Earthmaker had stretched it out,
he said: "Good!
You who saw of old this earth, this mud,
and made this nest, sing!
Telling old tales, humans will say of you:
'In ancient times, the being who was Meadowlark,
making the land and sticking it together in just that way,
built the nest from which the world was made.' "

Then Meadowlark sang—
sang a beautiful song about Earthmaker's creation.

And when they had stretched all the world out with ropes,
Coyote sang and sang, and by and by he stopped.
And Coyote said: "Now, you sing again."

And Meadowlark sang again:

"Lo, my world
where one may travel along the edge of the meadow—
lo, my world
where one may travel here and there, this way and that.
Lo, my mountains piled upon mountains.
Lo, my world where one may travel about!
I am one who will travel about in a world like that!"

Then the being who was Earthmaker sang—
he sang of the world which he had made.
He sang and sang; then, by and by, he stopped singing.
"Now," he said, "if this world were a very little bit bigger,
then that would be good.
Therefore, let us all stretch it."

Just then, Coyote said:
"Wait! I speak wisely!
It would be good to paint this world with something
so that it will be beautiful to see.
What do you two think of that?"

Then the being who was Meadowlark spoke.

He said: "I am a creature who knows nothing.
You two wise beings will, yourselves, be making this world,
thinking and talking together about it.
Then, indeed, seeing whatever is bad,
you two will make it good."

That was what Meadowlark said.

And then, Coyote said:
"Very well! I shall paint it with blood,
and, in this world, there will be blood,
and all kinds of creatures will be born with blood—
deer—all kinds of birds—all kinds of creatures—
all of them, without fail—
every kind will be born with blood in this world.
In various places, rocks, being red, will stay that way.
It will be, in this world, as if all is mingled with blood.

Then the world will be beautiful to look at.
Ay! What do you think of that?"

Meadowlark said: "What you say is good."

And then, Meadowlark went away.
And, as he left, he said:
"I am a creature who will travel like this."
And up and away he flew.

Earthmaker spoke.
"Please lie down here on your belly," he said.

"All right," said Coyote, and he lay on his belly.

He stretched out the land with his feet.
Pushing it out, little by little,
he stretched it out to where the sun rises—
first, he stretched it out to there.
Then, to the south, and to where the sun sets,
he stretched it out, little by little—
then, to the land beyond, to the North Country,
he stretched it out, little by little—
then, he stretched it out in all directions,
little by little.

Having stretched it all apart a little ways, not very far,
he said: "Enough!"

Then, Earthmaker looked up.
"Well," he said,
"It would be good
if this world were big enough to travel around in."

And then, by and by, he said:
"Please lie down again, and,
when you have stretched out on your belly,
don't look up. Don't do it!"

"All right," said Coyote. "I won't look up."
He lay down on his belly.

Stretching the land out, little by little,
toward where the sun rises,
he pushed it with his foot as far as he could.
Stretching it around, little by little,
toward the North Country,
he pushed it with his foot as far as he could.
Stretching it around, little by little,
toward where the sun goes down,
he pushed it with his foot as far as he could.

Stretching it around on all sides, little by little,
he pushed it with his foot as far as he could.
And then, he said: "Enough!"
and jumped up.
When he had jumped up, he stepped along hither,
to somewhere around here.

And then, Earthmaker was standing there alone.

Standing there, they say he went somewhere to the south.
He went travelling along.

Afterwards, going across the rim of the world
to somewhere near where the sun floats away,
he came elsewhere, into a different part of the country,
travelling always from one place to another.
And, when he had gone toward where the sun rises,
he came to a place where he had once turned aside before,
and he stopped and got things ready.

Then, he made creatures, two by two.

He made a pure white creature,
and then he made another one which, though also white,
was a little different.

He kept on, and made a black one;
then he made one, a little different, which was also black.

He made them only in pairs.

And then, he told off all the lands,
and, when he had counted them,
he gave to the lands the creatures he had made.

He said:
"This place will have this creature.
Each one of you will have a place to be.
These creatures will keep growing and growing
while many winters come and many mornings dawn.
They will grow and grow until the winters pass
and the mornings pass.
When they are done growing, they will be born.
When very many winters have gone by, they will be born.
Then they will have young, both female and male,
And when these are grown, they will also have young,
and when many winters have gone by,
there will be many creatures."

In this way, he gave to various creatures each its own place.

Then he spoke again.

"I have put all of you in this world.
Henceforth, this world will belong to you.
You will be creatures with names.
All of you will have names
and the places where you live will also have names.
Your places will all be places with names
and you will also have names.
You will be in this world,
and your descendents will fill it up.
Each and every one of them will have a name.

"Growing there,
as many winters pass and many days pass,
you will be grown,
and then this land will be yours."

He gave a different kind of creature to the land,
then he spoke once more again.

"You are creatures who speak differently—
creatures who look different.
You also will have a place of your own.
Your young,
growing weary,
wanting to live in another land,
going from this place,
will live there.
Being born there,
they will live on every bit of the land."

Then he divided out the lands among them.
"You take the land over *that* way,
And you others go to *that* country.
All of you various creatures will be called different things."

And then, later,
setting out another time,
he came back this way,
and, after he had travelled far,
and, when he had arrived at the middle of the world,
he made ready.

When he had made two beings, he put them there.

He said:
"You will grow and grow.
So, when a number of winters have gone by—
very many winters, many days have gone by—
you will be grown.
Then you will be born as human beings.

"And this country will have a name.
On the other side of this mountain is another country,
and that, also, shall have a name.

"But you will not be born soon."

Having set out from the center of the world,
he went away.
He kept going—going to certain places,
and, at those places where human beings were to live,
he stopped.

Then, he made things ready again.

He made two people,
then two more and then two more.
He kept count of them,
and, when he had counted them all,
he spoke.

"You will live here.
You and your country will have a name.
Living in a country that is little, not big,
you will be content.

"When I have gone hence,
you will grow and grow,
and, when a number of winters are past,
a great many winters, a great many days are gone by,
you will be grown.
And then, when you are grown,
you will be born.

"When you have been born,
different kinds of food,
all kinds of food will grow.
Then, after you are born,
you will be clever enough to survive."

Then he shoved them under the ground.

He made more people.
Then he spoke again.
"You will also have a small country."

And he spoke to all the people.

"You will not drive one another from each other's meadows,
saying: 'All right now! Clear out of our country!'

"You will call your countries by different names,
and you will also be differently named peoples.
Then, growing and growing—
when many days have passed—
many winters have passed—
when the day you will be born has passed—
then you will go on living, having children.
As other winters go by, and they get a little bigger,
going on like that,
going on growing,
after enough winters have passed,
you will have many children,
and there will be enough people.
Each and every one of your children will have a name.
In the same way,
this country will also have a name.
Every country will have a name.
If you go somewhere to have a look around,
and you say, as you set out,
'I'm going to such and such a country,'
calling it by name,
then everyone will know where you are going."

And, after that,
he picked out a creature from around here.
And he said:
"You, too, are going to be a human being
when several winters have passed.
When many winters have gone by,
you will be born.
Growing and growing,

you will get a little bigger each winter.
Though you are very small,
you will grow,
and, when winters have passed,
after many winters,
you will be grown.
And, when you are grown,
you will be born.

"You, too, will have a country there.
Your country will have a name.
You, too, will have a name,
and you will beget children.

"When they have gotten a little bigger,
your children will know the country,
having seen it all,
and having talked about it—
having given it a name.

"So, you will teach your children to name things:
'This place is called this;
that place is called that.'
Then, when you have taught them,
they will know what you know."

And, with the flick of a finger,
he sent the little being across the mountains.

As he was about to finish counting them all,
one still remained. He said:
"You, also, will be one who speaks another language.
You will beget a greater number of descendents.
You will be like the others,
and have a country of a certain size—
a big country.
It will be there where I used to wander about,
and you will, indeed, want for nothing."

With a sweep of his hand, he pointed out the land.

"The country I am speaking of
will be here forever,
and the last thing I shall tell you is to dwell here.
You are the last of my creatures.
Now that I have told you to dwell here,
I shall return to my own country and stay there.
If things are not just right in this country,
I shall make them so.
And, when I have done that, then, later,
you will be born."

Long before, Coyote divined all this.

He said:
"This earth is going to shift.
Since it is flat and thin, it will be an unstable world.
After the world has all been created,
then, by and by,
I shall tug on this rope from time to time,
making the earth shift."

"Now then, enough!" said Earthmaker.
"There will be songs—
there will always be songs,
and all of you will have them."

And after that, he sang—and sang—and sang;
then he stopped singing.

"These are the songs that you human beings will have,"
he said.
And then, he sang some other songs;
singing some other songs, he started off.

He went a long way
until he finally came to the middle of the world.
When he got that far,
he sat down and stayed there.

But, telling about the world,
Meadowlark sang very beautifully.
He was the first being created,
the first being to go across the meadows.
He was the being who saw the dry land,
very beautiful;
singing from the beginning—
a being who sang songs.

Then, travelling,
Earthmaker went past the middle of the world,
built a house,
and lived there.

He was there, at the ends of the earth.

That is all, they say.

II. The Adversaries

It was not so far from here—
just yonder, across from where the sun floats down—
that, long ago, in olden times,
an ancient being set forth.

"From hereabouts,
let us two gamble for the world,"
he said to Earthmaker,
"I, Coyote,
going along in this world,
will ruin it," he said.

"I speak for a good world," said Earthmaker.
"Let this be a good world!"

But Coyote said: "No!
Why are all these creatures born again after they die?
When creatures die, they should stay dead!
When anyone is dead,
why should he come to be walking around again?
You're just not going to arrange it that way!
I am the First Being of olden times,
and I say let the old people die when they die.
Someone who's dead is not going to wake up,
get to his feet, and stand there.
This world is made with Death in it.
If someone dies, then, afterwards,
he's not going to be breathing and walking about,
no matter *who* he is!"

That's what Coyote said.
And then, he said:
"I'm going to wander around
and take a good look at this world.
I'm not going to kill your people,
though you, their leader, is angry with me,

and though you are creating the world,
making it good,
it's not going to be just your world.
People will say,
'Coyote got the best of the Great Leader!' "

"That's the way they'll be talking
in every single country, to the ends of the earth.
And they're not going to laugh at me!
Nor are you, the Creator, going to laugh at me,
talking as if I didn't know how to do anything!"

Then Earthmaker grew angry.
"I will say how it's going to be," he answered.
"Let human beings not cease to exist.
From whatever cause they die,
let them be stretched out in the water,
and, in the morning, let them awaken.
Thus have I spoken!"

But Coyote shook his head.
"That's not the way it's going to be," he said.
"What you're saying is bad!
How is it that anyone who has died
could be going around the next morning?"

"Well, now," replied Earthmaker,
"if you talk like that,
you'll not be in this world for long."
And then, when they had spoken together,
Earthmaker and Coyote angrily departed from each other.

Meanwhile, there was a feast being planned.
Earthmaker was knotting strings.
At that time, long ago, he kept knotting strings
so he could send them out to several places,
to places where people lived.
He knotted strings.
He counted them out,
and sent them off to where people lived.

He counted out the knotted strings.
And finally the task was done.

Earthmaker talked to his people.
"Now, then," he said,
"You, there, go to *that* place!
And *you* go northwards!
And *you* go where people have gone to live!
And *you* go along beside here!
Go where there are people living!

"Go toward the sunrise!
Go toward the sunset,
down beneath the place
where the sun swims above the world!
Go, all of you,
and overlook no place where people live," he said.
And he spoke again:
"Let them all come and see me.
I must speak with them!"

Then the runners went,
and each one came to where he had been sent
at a different time.

And, when only a few days had passed,
people came from everywhere.
They kept coming and coming
until they had all arrived.
And, when they were all there,
Earthmaker addressed them.
"I speak for a good world," he said,
" 'Let this be a good world' is what I say!
But, when I say it, Coyote says 'No!'
Now, I am angry," said Earthmaker.
"My people,
you must all search with the utmost care
all around the borders of this world, even to the edge
where the waters encircle the land.

Everyone knows
that Coyote is the very one who will lose out.
Kill Coyote in whatever place you find him.
He is not good at all—he is bad!
He opposes me in everything!"

Then, Earthmaker said to one of the others:
"Go and tell your people now—
the ones who went from here."

And he said to another one:
"You who are the leader of the people
who live toward where the sun goes down—
you go and tell *them!*"
And he said to yet another one:
"You, the leader of those who went across from here,
go and tell *your* people!"

And he said to yet another one:
"you who come from where the sun rises,
go and tell *your* people!

In each and every country,
you must be alert!" he said.

They all said: "So be it!
We'll get on with killing Coyote,
and, when we've done it,
let's all keep a sharp ear
and, if we don't hear him howling
after four days have gone by,
then we will have really killed him!
Let's do it!"

"At the same time," said Earthmaker.
"All of you go and find every place
where Coyote has pissed or shat!
Don't any of you miss the places
where he has scratched the dirt.
Search all over the land."

"Very well," they said.

Meanwhile,
when his dispute with the Great Leader was over,
Coyote left.
He went off toward where the sun goes down,
He lifted his leg up against the bushes.
He scratched the ground with his hind feet.
He got onto a sandbar in the river then
and scratched with his hind feet.
He pissed on the sand.
He jumped on a clump of grass,
right there in the river,
and he pissed on that.

Then, he sprang out onto the bank and ran away.

He pissed on every kind of a thing there was
and scratched up the ground with his hind feet.
He went everywhere,
even up toward the land of the Spirit Masters.
Everywhere where there were bushes
he pissed on them.
Wandering everywhere,
he arrived to where the sun rises.

And after awhile, he came to the middle of that land.
Arriving, he got to the very center of it.
And, so far as that,
the people did not pursue him.

Meanwhile, the people stopped talking
and, afterwards, they went off in all directions.

Five of the leaders, along with their people,
set out in pursuit.
They spread out into each and every land.
And they travelled around,
looking for places where he had pissed,

where he had shat,
where he had scratched the ground.

They kept searching them out and destroying them—
every single place where he had pissed and shat,
rubbing them out until none could be seen.
They brought every last one of Coyote's droppings together.
And, when they had captured Coyote himself,
they brought him along with them.

Then all of the people came together in one place,
and they set out, leading him along.
They led him up to the banks of a river.
As they led him there, they found an islet
in the middle of the stream,
and they made him sit down on it.

"Here you will die!" they said.
"You who are so clever with words—
here you will starve to death!"
"Very well," said Coyote.
"Are all of you important men killing me
so that you alone will be leaders?
From each and every part of the world,
it will only be me that they laugh at!"

Coyote spoke to them like that.

"And *you*," said Coyote to Earthmaker,
"People from everywhere will say bad things about you.
They will say that *you* are the cleverest."

And, having spoken, Coyote remained silent.
And the others waded through the river
and clambered out on the shore.

"Now, then," said Earthmaker,
"Keep listening, all of you,
wherever you are.

If, after four days, you hear no sound from Coyote,
then he will have died."

Then they all went away.
Though they listened through the first night,
by morning there had been no sound from him.
Again, they listened until the next morning,
but there was no sound from him.

Meanwhile, Coyote was still on the islet.
After awhile, he shat. A gopher head crawled out.
"What shall I do?" Coyote asked the gopher head.
"Give me good counsel!"

"Well," said the gopher head,
"if you just stay here like you are, you will die!"

"Ah! That's the way you always talk to me," said Coyote.

Then, when he had strained again,
a bunch of dry grass crawled out.

"What *am* I to do?" asked Coyote.
"How shall I survive? Advise me well!"

"Why, you must just turn yourself into mist,"
said the bunch of grass,
"and then, when the mist rises
and floats up off the river at dawn,
it will carry you along with it
and bring you to the shore.
When you have called out,
then, from the midst of the high country,
the places where you have pissed,
where you have scratched up the ground—
even where you have lifted your leg against a clump of grass—
these places will answer you."

"Whenever this bunch of dry grass talks to me,
it always gives me good advice," exclaimed Coyote.

He stuck the grass back where it came from
and plugged it up with the gopher head.

Then, as day was breaking and it began to get light,
the mist floated up.
And he mingled with the mist.
The mist kept coming, and, before it floated away,
he drifted across to the shore.
Then he stopped in his tracks on the riverbank
and began to call out.
And it seemed as if there was an answer from far away.
Again, from somewhere else, there was an answer.
It was his piss—
it was the place where he had scratched with his claws—
it was the place where he had shat—
it was these that answered him.

Meanwhile, those people talked to each other.
"Since we didn't finish him off, we shall die," they said.
"We learned from Earthmaker
that Coyote would not call out for four days,
but now, though only three mornings have passed,
he is calling out."
They went to one another and said:
"He did, indeed, not die! He is, indeed, calling out!"

"You must track him down again," said Earthmaker.
"Come together, all of you,
from each and every part of the country!

"You might lose him. Go all out to find him!"
So they set out to track him down.
When they had gone everywhere, to every part of the country,
they finally caught up with him.
And they brought together any kind of thing
from where he seemed to have pissed,
or to have sat down.
And, when it seemed they had everything,
they captured him and started off with him.

They came upon a great tree.
They made him stand in the middle of it,
and they caused the tree to grow up around him.
He just kept standing there
while the tree grew up around him.

Then they talked together.
"Now," said Earthmaker, "let this be an end to him!
Let this be an end of his getting the best of us!
Let's not bother with him again.
If, in four days, he is not calling out here and there,
making a noise,
then, when darkness falls, we can assume that he is dead.
Then you will all tell each other about it."

Then they went off in all directions,
and, in every part of the country, they listened.

Meanwhile, Woodpecker came flying to where Coyote was.
He tapped on the tree.
He kept tapping and tapping,
and, when it grew dark, he went away.

Again, at daybreak, he flew back to the tree.
He tapped and tapped until he had made a hole through it.

Coyote saw someone moving through the hole.
He said: "Well, now, cousin!
Make this hole just a little bigger!

But Woodpecker stamped his foot and flew away,
never to return.

"I really messed *that* up!" said Coyote.
"I didn't do well at all!
Why didn't I just keep my mouth shut
and wait to see what would happen?"

So then, he started grunting and straining
until that gopher head crawled out.

"Well, what am I going to do?" asked Coyote.
"Don't lie to me! Just tell me!"

The gopher head said:
"There's nothing to do but just stay right here until you die!"

"No matter how many times you speak to me,
you have never once given me good advice," said Coyote.

Then, something else crawled out.

"What shall I do?" Coyote asked it then.
"Tell me all you can."

"What you should do," said the other,
"is to turn yourself into a mist,
and drift out through the hole until you are all outside.
If you do that, you will survive."

"Well," exclaimed Coyote,
"you certainly give me good advice every time!"

So Coyote turned into mist,
and drifted out through the hole
until he was all outside.

Then, just about daylight on the last morning,
he called out.
As morning came and the light moved over the hills,
he called out.

And, they say, the answers came back.
From every part of the land, the answers came back.
It sounded as it always had when Coyote howled.
In olden times, when many things could talk,
the places where he had pissed,
the places where he had scratched,
the places where he had rolled over and over,
where something had crawled out of him—
the places where all those things were

spoke up and answered him.
It sounded like a lot of them.
When he howled with his nose in the air,
they all spoke up and answered him.

And then, Earthmaker spoke again.
"Go visit the important men throughout the land,
and invite them here to me."

And his people went to invite them.
They went around,
and talked in every place to which they came.
And, afterwards, they came back.
And the leaders arrived, one by one.
They kept coming and coming
until they were as the trees in the forest.

At dawn, Earthmaker spoke.
"Are you all awake?" he asked.
"Is each and every one of you awake?
Listen, now, to what I have to say.
It will rain over the world.
It will snow and snow again.
Deep water will cover all the land.
You, my people, will make a boat.
You must believe what I tell you.

"It will truly happen. I have said enough!
It will rain,
and, when all these mountains are deep under water,
then Coyote will be no more!
And then, my people, only you will survive!"

"Very well, they said, and they set to work on the boat.

Meanwhile, Coyote disguised himself.
He didn't look like a coyote.
He mingled with the other people,
but they didn't recognize him.

They kept working through the winter.
The boat was not yet burnt out.
They worked, those people!
As the winter was about to set in again,
the boat was almost burnt out.
It snowed, but they kept at it.
As they stuck to the task,
it began to rain.
When they had worked through the second winter,
the task was done.

Be on the alert, all of you," said Earthmaker.

"Indeed we will," they said.

"Coyote might show up! You must always be on guard!"

"Very well," said one of them.
"I'll be always on guard!"
It was Coyote who spoke,
but the others didn't recognize him.

"I'll recognize Coyote," said Coyote.
"I'll tell you if he comes around," he said.
It was Coyote who spoke.

"Very well," said Earthmaker.

It rained.
Water came in and flooded the houses.
In the boat, they began to float.

"Are you the only ones here?" asked Earthmaker.
"Coyote isn't here, is he?"

"Only we ourselves are here," they answered.

The boat floated up. It rained.
All of the mountains were deep under water.
The world was water.

After they had floated about for awhile,
they saw land.
And they came to rest on Yakúkim Mountain.

Then, when they had gotten out of the boat,
Coyote said: "I'm the one who saw this land!"

Thereupon, that Great Person,
taking a long look at Coyote,
bowed his head and said nothing.
For it was that Coyote, who had slipped into the boat,
and none of the people had recognized him.

"You have great power," said Earthmaker,
"and, therefore, I shall hunt you down no longer.
Though I have tried for a long time to kill you,
I cannot. You have conquered me!"

Meanwhile, Coyote, who had jumped out of the boat,
trotted a little way down the ridge.

"All of you, go wherever you wish," Earthmaker told his
        people.
And, after that, he set out,
and went away from them down the mountain.
And, afterwards, when he got down below,
he stayed there.

III. Love and Death

They say that Coyote went to the very place
where Earthmaker had betaken himself before.
He went over to the land where the day begins,
and, always going up and over the ridges,
he circled back this way, moving ever southward.

He got closer, then,
and he came at last to where that man was living
who had been angry with him. It was Earthmaker.
At that time, he was dwelling there with his wife.

"Well!" said Coyote, "my brother,
"you seem to be headed for a bad marriage, living with a wife.
How is it that a good-looking woman
would come to marry an ugly man like you?
You don't even look like a person.
And here I am, a handsome man without a wife!"

After that, he moved in with them.

"If you can find me a woman anywhere,
give her to me," said Coyote.
"I have always had great will power.
The first time I sleep with these two women
and they start playing around with me,
I won't move a muscle."

"If you do that, you'll just wake up in the morning with wives,"
        said Earthmaker.
"And then, all the next night,
if you want to bother them, you can just go ahead and do it."

"I will not move!" declared Coyote.

So, in the middle of the night,
Earthmaker carried two elderberry flutes across
and laid them alongside Coyote.

They turned into women.

Then, when it was almost dawn,
Coyote woke up and snickered, "hn! hn!"
He played around with them, hugged them, kissed them
and whispered in their ears.

But, when daylight came,
the two women had disappeared.

"Coyote is who I am," he said.
"Indeed, I'm no good for anything at all!
A very bad Coyote!
Why don't I believe it when someone tells me something?

"If I had believed, everything would be fine
but now, I'm without a wife.

"I won't do it again!
I'll believe whatever anybody tells me."

So, they stayed there,
hunting all kinds of deer, ducks—anything to eat.
Killing them, eating them, they stayed there.

Then, Earthmaker, who was going hunting,
got his bow ready and left.
But Coyote stayed home.

When the Great Being came back,
he didn't know Coyote.
He didn't recognize him as Coyote.
As he was thinking it over, he pondered:
"That doesn't look like Coyote.
This fellow must have come from somewhere or other,
wandering around, looking for a place to live."

Then Earthmaker didn't think any more about it,
and they both stayed there.
They lived by netting salmon.

Other people came and lived there.

Then, a stranger came along,
and, when they had roasted fish—salmon—
they gave him some, and he ate it.
And later, when he had eaten, he got up and went away.

Coyote said:
"Look here! He wasted some of the fish he was eating!"
And Coyote gathered up the food which the stranger had
          dropped
and ate it.

"Everyone take a taste," said Coyote.
"Don't you think this tastes very good?"
He handed bits of it around to one person and another.

"It tastes wonderful!" they said.
"That must have been Salt Man!
Let's all go chase him down and kill him!"

So they chased him. They ran. They followed his tracks.
Even though he had just then left, they couldn't find him.

"Call on all your power!" said Coyote.
"Do your best! Set out after him!"

They went in pursuit.

"He might outrun us!" said Coyote.
"Take heart! Keep after him!"

They ran up to the top of a mountain
and looked all around,
but he was nowhere to be seen.

"Keep after him with all your strength," said Coyote.
"He might do us harm! Stay after him!"

They ran down the first mountain and up another one,
and, when they had taken a look around,
they quickly went down into the valley below.
The stranger, just a little bigger than a tall tree,
was far away and running.

"Now, then," said Coyote,
"stretch yourselves to the limit. Stay after him!
He seems to be getting away from us!

"Now, it does, indeed,
look as if he's gone further on over the ridge.
He seems to have left us far behind!"

Coyote outran everyone else.

"Do the best you can," he said.
They were all in hot pursuit.

They came to the edge of the valley,
but the stranger had already run across it.

"Use your power! Use your power!" said Coyote.
"He may outrun us yet!"

Coyote reached the middle of the valley.
"Now, then," he said, "it looks like he may get away from us!"

Then, raising his bow, Coyote shot an arrow
which seemed to travel swiftly to its mark.

It hit the stranger in the calf of the leg.
Pierced by that very arrow,
he broke all to pieces.

And so it was that Coyote killed the Salt Creature.

Then all the others caught up and Coyote spoke to them.
"When humans tell stories,
they'll say:
'Coyote killed Old Man Salt long ago,
after he had outrun everyone else.'
And people will come here from everywhere to gather salt.
This is where they'll come to get their salt."

And, when he had spoken, they set out for home.
They kept travelling to their own country.
They kept travelling on their old familiar trails.
They kept travelling until they got there.
And then, they stopped netting fish,
and went their separate ways.

Another time later, Earthmaker spoke.
"It is bad to have all these different kinds of creatures!
It is bad because they kill one another.
I'm going then," he said.

But Coyote remained there, silent.

"If all these creatures disappear,
then some others will live in this land," said Earthmaker.
"It's not good that all these creatures are killing each other.
It must stop!"

But Coyote said nothing.

He had a child, a boy, a big boy.
Coyote never let him crawl out of the house
but made him always stay home.
That was the way it was.

Now, Earthmaker said:
"Human beings, people with names, will live here.
There will be human beings.
And, when men want to take a wife,
they will take a wife.

But, when they are married,
they won't do anything with their wives."

Then, in a little while, Coyote spoke up and answered him.
"That which you say is bad!
Why will we not make it so that men and women hug and kiss,
and tickle one another and laugh and feel good?
When people get married, they should make love
and then, a little later,
they should lie down together and feel good!
And then, when they have finished lovemaking,
they should laugh a lot and talk to each other.
But if they never hug and kiss each other
but just go to sleep and get angry with each other—
if that's the way they do, then that's bad.
It's just not going to be that way!"

Meanwhile, Earthmaker listened in silence
and, when Coyote had finished, he spoke again.
"People will have children," he said.
"When, indeed, they want to have a child,
then they will lay something down between them
and they will say:
'You're going to be a girl,' or
'You're going to be a boy.'
When they have said what it is to be
and have laid it down between them,
then, when they wake up in the morning,
there it will be, not small and reasonably clever.
And so then, the women will not suffer
but will go about having children."

Meanwhile, Coyote listened and said nothing.
But when Earthmaker had finished speaking,
Coyote said:
"Women, weeping, straining, will give birth,
and later, after a while, they will have children.
And some of them will die,
and some of them will live."

And Earthmaker spoke again.
"Maidens will come together with men
only after they are married,
and unmarried men will sleep with women
only after they are married."
Thus spoke Earthmaker.

But Coyote started to speak.
"Indeed, women without husbands will have children.
As maidens, they will have children.
If they step across Coyote's piss,
then, as maidens, they will have children!
And the young lads, the men, ogling the women,
will laugh and talk and come together with them.
And the women without husbands will go fucking along the
        trails,
and they will have children.

"When a woman with child comes along,
then the lads will laugh and talk and feel wonderful."
Thus spoke Coyote.

Earthmaker spoke again.
"When people die, after they are dead,
they will be laid over into the river,
and, when they have lain there,
they will come to life again."

But Coyote answered him.
"When people die, they shall be dead
and they will be buried under the earth.
Indeed, the dead will not be going here and there in the
        morning.
When they are dead, they will be dead.
When women are bereaved, they will be bereaved
and they will mourn.
They will put pine-pitch on their heads,
and on their faces also.
They will weep and smear themselves with pitch
and make a terrifying noise.

But then, indeed, forgetting,
they will marry another man
and so they will feel very well again.
And men will do the same way.
A man, widowed for the third or second time,
will take himself a wife again
and, having married many times,
he will feel very well again.
A woman, too, many times bereaved,
still will take another husband
and all will be well.
Now, a leader should really say what is good!
But you, Earthmaker,
are not speaking for human contentment and joy!
But I speak for a world where men can laugh
and feel good and come to take delight in themselves
and in the women they care for.
So then, an old man,
flirting and playing around with a young woman,
should feel like a lad again.
And women should feel that way too.
I, too, am a great man
and what I say is very good!"
Thus spoke Coyote.

Then Earthmaker said nothing,
but he thought to himself:
"You, Coyote, have overcome me in everything;
so then, without my saying so,
let there be Death in the world."

And after that, Earthmaker got his things together,
and then he started off.
He set two scouring rushes on either side of a rivulet,
and then he came away hitherwards.

Not long after Earthmaker had left,
Coyote said to that fine son of his
whom he had never sent to do anything:
"Go and fetch some water!"

And the boy went to do it.
And then he went down to the water.
Those rushes were changed into rattlesnakes,
and they bit him, and that child died.

Then Coyote cried out.
"May I never say such things again!
Come back! Let there be no death in the world!
You must make my son come back to life!
Come back! I will never say such things again!
From now on, I will always pay heed to what you say!"

He ran after the Great One,
who paid him no mind but kept on coming hitherwards.

Coyote pursued him, but could not overtake him,
and he turned back.

"I am full of grief!" he said.
"In spite of the very many times I have won out over him,
he has done this to me! He has killed my child!"

Then Coyote stopped in his tracks.
"I will chase him no longer," he said.
"I will never catch up with him."

IV. Coyote the Spoiler

Now, Earthmaker came along this way
and, after he had walked for a while,
he crossed over a river and arrived there at the Pissing Place.
He went along the side of the hill beyond.

There was a sweathouse across the river—
the house of the Pissing Women
who rushed forth from time to time
and massacred the people roundabout.
Whenever someone came along,
they swooped down on him from their sweathouse
and killed him!

They looked out and saw Earthmaker
and they shot streams of piss at him across the river.
But he managed to get safely over the ridge
by sticking his flint-flaker into the ground.
That way, he kept going along until he was out of danger.

He went along
until he came to where the Mink brothers were living
and there he camped for the night.

In the morning, those two youngsters spoke.

"Why don't you help us set our trap?" they asked.
"Whenever we set it, the creatures always escape from it.
Why don't you set it for us?"

So Earthmaker went down and set the trap
and, when he had done so, he said:
"Don't say anything, you two, about what you've seen.
Keep your mouths shut and take off after those Pissing
        Women.
Grab up some of that grease there and take it with you.

When you get to the Pissing Women's sweathouse
and they have crawled in to sweat,
then throw it down through the smokehole
and run away as fast as you can!
And when they breathe in the smell of that grease
they will suffocate."

"All right!" said the Mink brothers.

And Earthmaker went away.

Now, the two Mink boys kept watch
and, in the morning, just as the sun was rising,
a condor was circling overhead.

Then, the younger brother said:
"There's a condor circling around—
something must be caught in our trap!"

Then they jumped up
and, hurrying along, they ran down to it.
As the condor,
who was going to carry the trapped thing up into the sky,
was just half way to it, the brothers ran up.
And after they had sprung up to where it was,
they cut it in two.
They saved back only the part toward the tail
and threw the rest of it up into the air.
Milk, dripping down, dripped on those two as they looked up.
Drops of milk fell on their mouths.
Drops of white milk fell on their chins.
Drops of milk were on their breasts.

And then, as it got along toward evening,
the Mink brothers took the grease
and carried it along to the Pissing Women's house.

Just at dark, those women were sweating
and dancing the bear dance.
They were terrible to see!

The boys flung the grease in through the smokehole
and then they ran away.

And then that sweathouse caught fire
and burnt to the ground.

Those two Mink brothers didn't stop running
until they got back to their home.
They stayed there.

All this time, Earthmaker was travelling along.
He arrived in Nearby Valley where the Crow brothers lived.
He made camp there.

Then those two brothers said to him . . .
"Elder brother, you'd better sharpen our knives for us.
Having them dull doesn't seem to do us any good.

So he sharpened the beaks on those two Crow brothers
and, after he had camped out there for awhile,
he walked away.

As he came walking along,
the pet porcupine of the Two Boys Who Stab People in Boats
was lying up on top of a rock.
He was a pet who always saw everything, they say,
but he didn't see Earthmaker!

Earthmaker dodged down out of sight
and got himself under the rock,
and having reached up,
and having grabbed the porcupine,
and having killed it,
and having tucked it into his belt,
he took himself silently away.

Meanwhile, the two boys just kept on talking with each other.
And then they took a look at the knife they used
to cut off people's heads with.

They said, as they were talking together:
"This is the kind of a thing we two always use
when we go around cutting off people's heads!"

The Great Being stepped down to where they were,
and, when he had gotten there, he stood on the bank of the
        river,
and they saw him.

Those two started to hide, but they couldn't.
Earthmaker saw them.
"Hey, you two, get me a boat!" he said.

The two boys pushed the boat out of the water,
but, when they got it partway on the bank,
they couldn't push it any further.
"Jump on in from where you are," said one of them.

He climbed down the bank
and started to jump into the boat from the bank of the river.
But, just as he was about to jump,
the boys moved the boat a little
so that he might slip and fall,
and then they could kill him.

That was the way they always did it—
so that people would slip and fall
and the boys could attack with their knives
and cut their heads off.

So, they crouched to spring on him,
but, as he jumped aside, he said:
"Now, then! Let me have a look at your knives!
Which of your knives is better?"

Then the boys stood up,
took out their knives,
and gave them to him.

Earthmaker took them and said:
"Well! You certainly seem to have very fine knives!
I'm going now.
I suppose you two know your way around in this country.
You must feel at home in all these mountains around here.
On this mountain here, in olden times,
the people came out of a boat and left it there.
They abandoned the boat.
Before then, deep waters covered all this land,
all these mountains roundabout."

Then, as he spoke,
Earthmaker took one of the knives and pointed all around.
He pointed toward each and every part of the countryside.

Then he stuck one of the knives in their throats
and cut their heads off. He killed them both.
And after that, he put them on his back
and lifted them up out of the boat.

Now, there was an earth oven there nearby
with a fire burning round it.

He laid the two boys down there,
and pulled off their pissers.
He put the two bodies into the oven,
and, when they were covered up,
when they were completely covered up,
he laid a trap by bending their pissers over,
and he went away.
After he had done something with those two bodies—
when he had covered them up—
he went away.

And then,
he came to where the grandmother of the two boys lived.
He took the porcupine which was tucked under his belt
and flung it across at her.
"Take that porcupine, bake it in the ashes and eat it!"
he said to her as he threw it across.

But she threw it back at him and said,
as she threw it,
"Take that porcupine, bake it in the ashes and eat it!"

But Earthmaker picked it up and threw it back again.
"Take that porcupine, bake it in the ashes and eat it!"
          he said.

But she threw it back again and said: "Bake it and eat it!"

So then, he spread the embers apart
and laid the porcupine down into them.
He covered it over,
stretched himself out with his back to the fire,
and went to sleep.
He usually slept with his back to the fire.
In truth, only a shadow of his real self was there—
a log, a rotten log.

That old woman reached across
and picked up her stone pestle,
and, when she had taken careful aim,
she bashed the log with it.
She made the log burst and fly all to pieces.

"Well, well!" she said,
"I didn't think that was really you there.
I really did believe that it was some old thing!"

The rotten log did look like him,
but Earthmaker, who had been lying with his back to the fire,
had already gone away to some other place.
Only his shadow remained there.
Though he seemed to be lying with his back to the fire,
it was really only his shadow.

Later on, the old woman jumped up and ran away.
"I suppose he must have eaten my two grandsons long since!"
          she said.

Talking to herself like that,
she ran to the trap and stooped down,
and, at that very moment, she was caught in the trap.

Thus Earthmaker killed off all three of them.
But he paid no mind to that, and went on his way.

After he had travelled for a long time,
he came to where Grouse Old Woman lived.
He made camp there, and then went on again in the morning.

He set out and went along
until he came to Grizzly Old Woman's house.
When he got there, he had her two cubs tucked under his belt.

"Singe the hair off these squirrels and let's eat them,"
          he said.

Then, while she gave him a bewildered look,
he lay down with his back to the fire.
But, in fact, he had already gone away
and it was only a shadow that seemed to be sleeping there.

She grabbed up her digging stick
and brought it around to hit him,
but what she hit was a log.

"I guessed that it wasn't you but something else!" she said.
"Well, well! I'm sure you'll outlive us all!"
And she set out to find him,
whirling her skirt so that it fluttered about.

Then the countryside caught fire.
It seemed as if the fire swept over the land everywhere.
Everywhere, it seemed.

And then, Earthmaker asked of Water:
"How is it with you?"
and Water answered:
"I'm boiling and bubbling. I'm very hot!"

And he asked Rock:
"How is it with you?"
and Rock answered:
"I'm hot, and from time to time I burst!"

And he asked Tree:
"How is it with you?"
and Tree answered:
"I'm burning mightily, and I'll stay very hot!"

And he asked Milkweed:
"And how is it with you?"
and Milkweed answered:
"When the fire has come and gone, I'm left standing behind!"
And Milkweed crawled out into the midst of the fire
and stayed there.

The country kept burning until it was all burned up.
And when it had cooled,
Grizzly Old Woman kept following Earthmaker's tracks.
She kept tracking him all around, going all around.
But she gave up and went home.

Earthmaker travelled along, coming this way.
He climbed up to the top of a ridge.
"Well," he said, "it seems to me that this sugar pine
is something for human beings to eat.
So people will have to climb up,
throw the cones down,
and gather them."
He said to the sugar pine:
"You're going to be short and low-limbed."

He left and came on further this way.

But Coyote, angry, came along after him.
When he got to where the sugar pine tree was, he said:
"I wonder how in the world this tree got to be so short!"
And he pissed on it.

"Now most of the pine cones are high in the top of the tree
so that when people see them,
they won't be able to climb up to them," he said.
And he went on his way.

Now, when Earthmaker had come along this way for awhile,
he sat down and took a look around.

"Here is where people will fish for salmon with nets," he said.
"They will stretch the nets wide,
and throw them in, time after time.
And, on the other side of the river,
they will do the same thing."

He set out again,
and travelled and travelled,
coming always this way, they say.
And there, at the Place of the Little White Root,
he sat down and ate little white roots for lunch.
And, when he had eaten, he got to his feet;
he stood awhile and gazed all around him.

He started off downhill,
and kept going and going
until he came to Hanýlekim Valley.

"Well, I still have this beautiful country left," he said.
"While Coyote is spoiling the world,
here I'll make a place where old people may reawake!
A place where human beings—old human beings—
may bathe and become young again!"
And he made a little hill.
He kept climbing up it as fast as he could
until he got to the top.

"Here," he said,
"old people who are about to die
will climb and climb until they get to the very top,
and then, when they have bathed in this pool,

they will be young again!"
And then, he went away.

He set out from there,
and crossed over to where the sun comes up.

But Coyote was going around here and there.
He saw the hill and said:
"I wonder why this hill is the way it is."
He looked it all over.
He stared at it for a while.
"I think I'll just piss on it!" he said.

He took another quick look at the hill,
there in the middle of the valley,
and he pissed on it.

Then that hill toppled over,
and, when it had fallen,
it broke open,
and the water spilled out into the house of the Great Serpent.
And the water flooded everything
until it had filled up the whole valley.
And the valley is filled with water to this very day!

"People will say of me, talking and laughing:
'Long ago, Coyote pissed on Óskypem Mountain
and made it tumble down!
In those olden times, Coyote was very powerful.
He got the best of Earthmaker and made him angry!'
That's what they'll say when they talk to each other,
and they'll laugh.

"I will be Coyote forever!"

That's what Coyote said.

Then, they say,
. he went along by where Óskypem Mountain had been.

And, when he had howled "Wowowowowowo!",
he ran away. He said: "People will talk about me!"

And he went away from there.
He was not thinking about anything at all
because all his work was done.

That's all, they say.

Tales of
Old Man
Coyote

Coyote and the Wind Creatures

A very large group of brothers was living together.

From their village,
they heard the faraway sound of women singing.
And the men in the village told each other of two very
      beautiful women who lived in the North Country.
And the men went courting these two fine women—
the daughters of Old Man Parsnip's brother.

Now, on a high pass which lay between, lived the mountain-
      tossing wind creatures.

No one who had heard the women could make it over the pass.

"Someone must do his best to get up and over," said the
      villagers.

So then, one man got all his trappings together and went.
He camped by a little spring on the mountainside,
and in the morning he set out again;
but, as he went quickly up, the wind creatures killed him.

One of his brothers set out to follow him.
"He didn't come back. He's in weird and mysterious country.
I'm going to seek him out and be with him," said the brother.

"Well," said the eldest of the group, "go ahead, but be wary and
      alert!
And tell us that you'll just go far enough to find out what has
      happened.
Then, on whatever day you name,
We can be on the lookout for you to return."

"All right," said the brother. "I'll do just as you asked.
It seems likely that my brother didn't get through the pass yet.
So, I'll follow him,
and, if I survive, I'll be back when seven days have gone by.
But, if I die, it will take me longer than seven days and seven
     nights!
If that's the case, then just say: 'He's dead!' "
So he left.
And he went along until he came to the spring where there
     was a little hut built,
and he made camp there.
In the morning, when he had eaten breakfast, he set out again
and travelled quickly up.
He saw where his brother had been killed.
He kept climbing up beyond,
and, when he had gotten just a little bit further,
the wind creatures killed him.

Now, the villagers stayed there in their houses
waiting for him to come back.
They kept waiting, for he had told them: "I'll be back."

But the seventh day passed. "He'll come tonight," they said.
But he didn't come and the day had passed.

"Well! He must be dead!" said Magpie.
"I, myself, will go. All of you stay here!"

"All right," they said.

In the morning, he spoke.
"I'm off to fight with some kind of being or other. I'm going.
Now, my people, don't expect me at any special time.
I'll come back on the day I want to come back—
that is, if nothing gets the best of me."

Then he decked himself out in his finery.
He put on a good netted cap and benecklaced himself with a
     new necklace.

He put on his yellowhammer feather headstall.
He stuck tremblers in his hair and sprinkled himself with
    goosedown.

"Now then," he said, "I'm going. All of you stay here."
And he went.
He kept going until he came to the camp by the spring,
and then he bedded down there for the night.

Later, when he had slept, awakened in the morning, and had
    his morning meal,
he set out again.

He sang.
When he got just a little way from his campfire,
he sang, swinging his body from side to side.

And he kept singing, turning first to one side and then to the
    other.
He sang.

Meanwhile, from away off somewhere, Coyote heard him.
"Ah! What could that be?" he asked himself.
"Well, well. It sounds very fine!
I think I'll just go see who it is!"
So he trotted off toward it.

Now, when he got about halfway to where the singing was
    coming from, he called out.
"What strange part of the country am I in,
with my head bowed down, about to sing?
What strange part of the country am I in,
looking all around, getting ready to sing?"

Coyote was talking.

"Well, now, cousin! How beautifully you sing!
But what part of the country are you going to?
Just tell me, where could you be going?"

Magpie sat down on a rock and stayed there.
And Coyote stood there and spoke to him.
After awhile, Magpie answered.

"Here I am, not doing anything," he said.
"A little while ago, two of my brothers were travelling around
     in this part of the country.
I'm searching for them, but I haven't found them.
Why do you want to know?"
It was Magpie who said it.

Then Coyote spoke.
"Who is following you?" he asked.
"If you're going all by yourself, then people won't see you and
     talk to you."

"I'm going alone," said Magpie. "Stay here!"
He talked to Coyote, trying to get him to stay back.

But Coyote shook his head. "No," he said.
"Why are you going around by yourself?
I'll go with you, cousin.
I'm one who mingles with important men.
If you're going where there are lots of people,
then it's proper for the two of us to go.
If you go alone, then nobody's going to notice you.
But, if I'm with you, then people will say:
'This is a good man, travelling with a notable personage!'
So, I'm going with you.

"All right, then," said Magpie.
"If you want to go, then you're going to go.
But hang onto my belt when we get a little further up from
     here.

Then, when the sun had risen a little, they set out.
When they had gotten a little way along, Magpie said:
"Take hold of my belt and go up with your eyes closed.
Only when we reach the pass can you take a peek.
But you mustn't peek now. Don't do it!"

"All right," said Coyote. "I'm not peeking.
"I'll climb up with my eyes closed until we get to the top."
Coyote spoke.

With Coyote forbidden to peek, the two of them started up the
    mountain.

Going along with his eyes closed, Coyote climbed up.

As they got almost to the top, Coyote said to himself:
"I wonder why he told me to keep my eyes closed.
I don't think I would die if I just took a look!
Since Magpie has his eyes open, why am I going along with
    my eyes shut?
We'll be better off if we're both looking around!
I want to see everything too!"

That's the way Coyote was thinking to himself.
"If he looks back to see if my eyes are still shut.
I'll just say that they are!"
He thought it all over as he went along,
and then he took a peek.
Then, when they had gotten almost to the top,
it seemed as if something moved over him and touched him.
He wanted desperately to see it.
"What kind of a creature could that be?" he asked.
He opened his eyes wide and looked all around him.
Something unseen, something that would not let him see it
grabbed him, held him and killed him.

Magpie took never a look backward, but went on his way.

He kept going until he came to where there was a house—
a house across on the other side of a river.
When he got to the river, he made camp.
And afterwards, in the morning, when he had gotten up,
    he sang.
He kept singing and singing, then later he spoke.
"Bring me a boat!" he said.

Then Old Man Parsnip said: "Take him a boat!"

Two men went down to the boat,
and, when they got there, they took it across.

"You two aren't the ones I was talking to," said Magpie.

So the two went back across again.
They got out of the boat and went up to the house.
"He told us: 'You two are not the ones I spoke to,' " they said.

Old Man Parsnip said to them:
"He talks like a mysterious and frightening man!
You must all well believe me!
Now then, *you* two take the boat."

Two women, then, went down to the river,
and, when they got there, they went across with the boat.

"You're not the ones I was talking to," said Magpie.

They went back, and, when they had gotten out of the boat,
they went up to the house.
"He told us: 'You're not the ones I was talking to,' " they said.

Then Old Man Parsnip said: "He talks like a powerful and
        mysterious man!
All of you, do the best you can. Be very cautious!"

Then he said: "Now, *you* two take the boat."

Two middle-aged men, then, went down to the river,
and, when they got there, they took the boat across.
When they got across, Magpie said:
"Did I call you two?
It's not you two that I was talking to!"

So *those* two went back.
And, when they had crossed over, they went up to the house.
"He told us: 'It's not you two that I was talking to,' " they said.

"All right," said Old Man Parsnip.
"He talks like a strange and powerful man!
Everybody, do all you can to survive!
You two take the boat."

Two middle-aged women, then, went down to the river and
took the boat across.

When they got across, Magpie said:
"Did I call you two?
It's not you two I was talking to!"

So the two women crossed the river again, got out of the boat
and went up to the house.
They said: "He told us that we weren't the ones he was talking
to."

"Well, then," said Old Man Parsnip, "maybe it was *you* two!
So why don't you two come on out?"

Then it was that those two beautiful women—
those daughters of Old Man Parsnip's brother—
those women who seldom came out of the house
and who never went anywhere—
did come out, and they took the boat across.

Then Magpie sang, swaying from side to side.
Loud and fast he sang, that Magpie.
When those two women had gone down to the boat—
when they had crossed over to his side of the river—
he said: "That's *right!* You two are the ones I invited to come
over!"

He got into the boat and, when they had crossed the river,
they went up to the house and crawled in.
Those two women made a lot of good things to eat.
They fed him,
and, when he had eaten his fill, he just stayed there.

He married those two women.

A few days later, Magpie set out.
He started back to his village,
and the two women went with him.
They went along over the mountain pass
and, as they came down the other side,
there lay Coyote's bones, thrown around.

The wind creatures didn't bother people who were
        returning—
only for those who were going the other way were the beings
        frightening.
But Magpie was, himself, very frightening!
He was stronger than beings like that.
He conquered them and went on down the mountain.

He came on, together with the women.
They gathered up Coyote's bones and brought them along.

Then they saw Magpie's brother. He was nothing but bones,
        scattered around.
They picked them up and went on down the mountain.
About halfway down, they saw the other brother's bones lying
        scattered around.
They picked them up and came along.
They came along until they got to the spring,
and then, they made camp for the night.

They had supper and went to sleep.
Then, in the morning, when they had awakened and finished
        breakfast,
they set out again.

Now, they had put Coyote's bones in the spring the night
        before.
Then they travelled on homewards, carrying the bones of
        Magpie's brothers,
and in the evening, when they got there, they put the bones in
        the water.
The next morning, the brothers rose up out of the water and
        came into the house.

And so, long ago, they were all there together again.

In the meantime, Coyote woke up the next morning in the
    spring and took a look all around.
"My cousin seems to have left me behind," he said to himself.
"I've been sleeping for quite a little while. He really seems to
    have left me!
Well, now. I wonder where all my cousins live.
I'll just see. I'll go have a look around.
I'll circle all around from where the day begins to where the
    sun goes down."
He turned as he spoke and made a sweeping gesture.

He was, indeed, all alone.

He set out in this direction.
After he had gone a long ways,
he came onto a man carrying a buckskin bag,
carrying it tied up tightly.

"Well, who can that be?" said Coyote to himself.
"He seems to be a big man, maybe even as big as me.
I'm going to ask him to fight!" thought Coyote as they came up
    to one another.

"Hello. Where are you off to?" Coyote asked.
"You look like a really big fellow!"
It was Coyote who spoke.
"Let's fight, cousin! We're about the same size."

"No, no!," said the other. "None of that fighting!
I'm tired from carrying this bag around.
I've come a long way. I'll be going now."

"What's that you're carrying?" asked Coyote.
"Let me have a look at it."

"No," said the other. "You can't see it. It's something bad."

"What's bad about it?" asked Coyote.
"I just want to see it. Show it to me!"

"No. It's magically powerful," replied the other.

"Tell me," said Coyote.
"If you'll tell me all about it, I'll let you go.
You can just go on your way. I won't bother you."

So then, the man spoke.
"I've come here from far away because I don't like to see bad
    winds blowing around.
These wind creatures bring lots of dire sickness when they
    blow on human beings
so that they all become ill.
Now, I'm going to put a stop to these wind creatures.
These wind creatures make everyone frail and weak.
These wind creatures make everyone cough and wheeze.
These wind creatures bring every kind of sickness.
These wind creatures cause great winds to blow,
and, when the wind blows over the land,
then people can't see what's going on around them.
These wind creatures bring lots of things that make people
    sick!
That's the kind of creature *they* are!
When they blow, they make people have sad and pitiful
    coughs!
So you see, I'm carrying these really powerful and magic
    creatures with me,
and I'm not going to let you see them."

That's what the man who carried the winds said.

"And so, I have come from far away, at the end of the world,
travelling about, carrying them in a sack—
all kinds of wind creatures—
The gusty creature, the whirlwind creature—
searching out every kind of wind creature.

I have travelled and travelled,
not for just a few days but for many days,
searching in all the country hereabouts,
grabbing them, tying them up in my bag,
catching sight of them in place after place,
tying them up in my bag,
going from one part of the country to another,
seeing others and tying them up
and then going to another country a little further along,
searching, never missing a single one,
grabbing up every kind of wind creature.
I think I have gotten them all now,
going around with my bag.
I really think I have them all!
And now, here I am, carrying them along.
When I have them all in my country,
then all these countries I have gone to, travelled around in
    and left from
will be safe and good.
Now, I think I've told you enough."

All this time, Coyote listened without saying anything.
He kept listening until the other had finished talking.
Then, he said: "All right! That's good!
But I think that if you gave *me* some of them,
I could also help make things very good.
If two people were doing what needs to be done,
it would be better all around.
You'd better give some of them to me, cousin.
I really am an important person!
It will be good if *I'm* doing this too!"

But the man who was carrying the bag of winds refused.
"No, no!" he said. "That would be bad!
It would make people feel terrible,
not only here but everywhere, if those ill winds were blowing.
When people have their meal all cooked and are eating it,
then up will blow a whirlwind,
picking up dirt and flinging it into their food.

That will be terrible! I don't want to see it happen!
I want to make this a good world!"

Thus spoke the man who was carrying the winds.
He was reluctant to give any of them to Coyote.

Coyote, meanwhile, who had said nothing,
was simply there, listening.
But, when the other had stopped talking,
Coyote started, again, to speak.

"That's really fine," he said.
"You seem to have it very well thought out indeed!
But then, I, like you, am also a thoughtful person.
Wherever I go, people consider me an able man!
And, indeed, I am! I'm a good thinker!
When I'm wandering around in the world,
many men and many women say:
'That's a good man, a real leader!'
It's the kind of thing they say whenever they see me.
So, you should give me some of the winds!
I'm a fellow who, like you, does good things.
I'm a fine fellow."

Hearing all this, the man with the winds stood there
        speechless,
but, after awhile, he spoke.
"Don't you believe what I told you?" he asked.
"I *said* that I wouldn't give you any of them,
and, I'm telling you now, I'm not *going* to give you any!
Travelling again, not just a few days but many days,
I have carried away the winds I have caught.
And, when, in some part of the country,
the winds start blowing,
making the dust whirl around
as if the winds were angry with the little twigs and leaves,
then I don't want to see the winds moving all kinds of rubbish.
When I have carried the winds away,
then this will become a good land."
It was the man who carried the winds who spoke.

Then, when Coyote had been there listening for awhile, he
   spoke.

"I tell you, I am not a man from somewhere else, a stranger,
asking you to give me some of the winds.
Indeed, there are plenty of people who would be dishonest,
who would try to trick you.
But I am your *cousin,* and *you* are *my* good cousin!
You've been in my thoughts for many days!
Who do you think is talking to you with words you can trust?
It's me, a good person, cousin,
and it's only you I'm always thinking of.
So then, give me some of the winds!
You'd better give them to me!"

The other was silent, thinking about it. He was angry.

Coyote kept listening, and, when the other did not answer,
Coyote spoke again.

"Do you hear? Hear me when I tell you!
Give me some of the winds!" he said.
"Don't you like for anybody—your brothers—
to help you out a little?
After all, brothers and cousins are not strangers!
It's very good for kinsmen to work together on whatever needs
   to be done.
Now, if you don't know how to take care of all the winds,
why don't you give me ten or so of them?
Don't look away from me!
Long ago, when I was very small, I actually visited you.
My father came on a friendly journey to visit your father,
and we stayed there and got to know all you children.
But, it seems, you don't remember that,
though *I* have *often* thought of *you*!
And now, you act as if you don't even know me!"

As Coyote was talking,
the man with the winds listened and said nothing.

After he had been there silent for awhile,
    he spoke.

"Oh, very well," he said.
"I'll divide them evenly with you.
Take them and go. Put them on your back, as I do,
and carry them out of this country!
If you want to have them, then just do it that way."

"But don't untie the bag and peek in while you're around here.
You mustn't do that! You mustn't untie it!
You must keep those winds where they are!"

"All right," said Coyote.
"That's what I'll do. I won't untie the bag.
I'm going to carry it away from here,
and, when I've carried it off to my own country,
I'll certainly not untie it there!
You say that you're bringing your winds home to your country.
Then I say that I'll take mine home to *my* country."

It was Coyote who was talking.

The man carrying the winds was very loath to give any away.
But there seemed to be no choice, so, with a feeling of defeat,
he gave Coyote some.
But, when Coyote demanded that he get half of them,
the man refused and gave him only a few.

"You go your way," he said, "and I'll go mine."

Then the man who had the winds got up and left.

After that, Coyote set out to come toward where we are now.
When he had come along a little ways,
he looked back over his shoulder.
"I wonder if there's anything to really be afraid of.
I think it would be well if I just took a look,"
he said to himself.
"I'll just untie the bag and peek in!"

He glanced over his shoulder again,
then he stood up and looked all around.
He got down on his knees and he untied it,
and, as he was untying it, he hung onto it tightly.
Then, when it was untied, he let the bag go.
And, as he let it go, the winds just rushed out with a whoosh
and swept him up into the Meadows Above.
And then, later, just his bones, stripped of flesh,
fell back down to earth.
And so, Coyote died.

And the wind was forever blowing,
making the trees fall,
and the wind creatures were going here and there,
always blustering, gusting, knocking down the tree people.
Long ago, in olden times,
when Coyote had let the wind creatures go,
they blew everywhere across the land.
That is the way Coyote spoiled the country
because the wind creatures have been here ever since.

Meanwhile, that man, the one carrying the other winds,
kept travelling until he got back to his own country
and, when he had got there with them, he let them go.
But there those winds were never very strong.
And, in those days long ago, he stayed there.

They say that's all.

Coyote and Muskrat

There was once a village where some people were living,
including many women.

The men went off hunting.
Later, they arrived home.
It was deer meat they were carrying back with them.

At dusk,
everyone ate supper and went to sleep.

In the morning, when they woke up,
the eldest of them said:
"Muster all of your spiritual power,
for you must kill deer and cure the meat,
and store it in the earth lodge for the winter.
This is a hungry world,
but that's the way it will always be."

When he had spoken, the others said:
"Yes! Since that's the way the world is,
then going hunting will keep us all in good health.
Let's do the best we can!"

Then, they all went off in various directions.

As it got along toward evening,
they all arrived back home.

One of them, who had stayed in the lodge,
was lying up against the wall inside.

A hunter, carrying a deer,
crawled up to the smokehole.
The man inside got up and took the deer from him.

Another hunter crawled up there,
carrying a deer,
and yet another.

The man in the house took them all,
and laid them down on the opposite side of the fire.
He took them from the hunters,
who carried the deer up to the smokehole.
He was a man who did that sort of work,
this one who stayed in the lodge.

Everyone kept arriving until they were all there.
When the deer had all been thrown down,
what a lot of them there were, indeed!
A pile of deer!

Meanwhile, the women leached acorns.

The men were crawling into the lodge.
Just as the last one crawled in—
just as he was standing at the top of the smokehole—
just as he stooped over to get in—
Muskrat made a lunge for him, grabbed him,
and, going at lightning speed,
jumped off the lodge and ran away with him.

Then, Muskrat laid him on the ground.
The man kept crying and crying.
But Muskrat killed him,
slung him on his back,
and carried him away.

While Muskrat was doing that to their kinsman,
the men just stared and said nothing.
They sat and listened while their kinsman was screaming,
and they were all afraid.
It was their eldest kinsman who was killed.

The women, too, having watched,
just went on about their business.

They said: "That's a terrifying creature!"
The women told each other that,
and the men said the same.

Muskrat carried the dead man away to his house.
His wife took the corpse from him, and put it down.
And then, skinning and preparing it,
she hung it up to dry.
"Good," she said.
"If you keep doing this, we two will have plenty of meat."

"Yes," he said.
"If I just keep on killing them,
I'll finally kill all those people off."

That's what Muskrat and his wife said, talking together.

Meanwhile, back at the village,
one of the men spoke.
"I wonder who this creature is," he said.
"He seems ghastly to us—
strong and invincible.
But we must do the best we can to survive."
It was the man who was now the eldest who said that.

Later, in the morning, when they had talked again,
they went off hunting.
And they arrived back home along toward dusk,
one by one, bringing home deer.
What a great many of them there were!

And, when they had all gotten back,
and the man in the lodge had taken the deer,
then the men kept crawling in until all but one were inside.

As the last man was creeping in on hands and knees,
Muskrat jumped out from behind the centerpost,
grabbed him,
carried him outside and laid him down.
The man was crying so that it was pitiful to hear.

Then, Muskrat killed him.
The men just sat there and watched, speechless.

Muskrat picked the dead man up and carried him away.
And, when he got home, he said to his wife:
"Killing people is what I'll be doing.
We'll have lots of meat!"

They skinned and prepared the meat,
and hung it up to dry.

At dawn, again, the village elder spoke.
"If this goes on, he will kill us all," he said.
"Indeed, that's what he seems to be doing.
But let's not despair!
Go to the mountain where you graze, everyone,
and graze as always."

"All right," said the men,
"but, since he's doing this to us,
what are we going to do about it?"

"Just pay no attention to him,
and go on as if nothing had happened," said the elder.

So, they trudged off in all directions,
kicking up the dust.

But the one fellow stayed there—
the one who always stayed and dressed the meat—
the one who always did the work.
The women helped him,
but they said nothing to him.

Later on, someone spoke to the elder.
"When the men come home at sunset,
and, after they all stand around here,
they crawl into the lodge.

Now, I wonder where Muskrat hides
before he jumps out and grabs one of them."
It was one of the women who said that.

Now, the women didn't go into the lodge all day.
They were grinding acorns,
preparing all kinds of food
for when the men came back in the evening.
So, there was no way
that the women could know where Muskrat came from
when he jumped out and grabbed people.

But the elder knew. He spoke.
"He stops behind where the spirit-post stands.
As the men arrive, he jumps out,
grabs one of them,
and runs away, carrying him in his arms."

"So *that's* it?" the woman said.

Later, the men arrived at the usual time,
just as the sun was setting.
They came carrying deer.
They kept coming and coming
until all had arrived.
They kept passing the deer into the lodge
until they had passed them all in.

Muskrat was up close behind the spirit-post.

Then, the last man crawled in.
And Muskrat, with wary grace,
grabbed him up and carried him out of the lodge.
And, when he had laid him down, he killed him.

He brought his quarry home,
and his wife took it from him.
She cut it into strips,
prepared it nicely, and hung it up to dry.
it was ghastly to see!

Again, on another morning,
the men went hunting.
"Don't be afraid of Muskrat," the elder told them.
"Get up and go to the mountains where you graze.
Go get whatever you need to survive."

The men said: "What else *can* we do?"
They went.

Now, Coyote was coming along, just at sunset.
He got to the village, sat down,
and, after awhile, he spoke to the women.
"Now, then," he said,
"you women, who are my new-found cousins,
must all do your best and make something to eat.
When we have eaten, I'm going to spend the night."

Then one of the women said:
"In fact, we haven't had much appetite.
We just sit around here feeling miserable.
Although we have done nothing wrong,
wherever our men go, Muskrat chases them down.
He kills our kinsmen without mercy.
So, we just stay here, weeping and mourning."

Coyote asked:
"Where does he keep watch from?
Where does he lay them down before he kills them?"

"He carries them to here," said the woman,
pointing to the place.

"I think he stands up close behind the spirit-post,
spying on the men," said the elder.
"But the men, themselves, do wrong.
They are so terrified that,
though they see the victim being killed,
and hear him cry out,
they do nothing about it."

"Ah," said Coyote, "he won't terrify *me*!
He won't make anyone scream while *I'm* watching!
Nobody is going to make anyone cry when *I'm* around!
Wait till I lay eyes on that Muskrat!
That will be when the sun gets down *there*, I suppose."

"Yes," said the elder. Just before sundown.

So then, Coyote went off up the hill a little ways,
and, when he got there,
he strained, and shat out a gopher's head.
he said: "Talk to me! How shall I kill Muskrat?"

"Maybe *he'll* kill *you*!" answered the gopher's head.

"Aw, you're always talking to me that way," said Coyote,
and he gave the gopher's head a kick
and sent it rolling down the hill.
Then, when he had strained again,
he shat out a bunch of dry grass,
and he asked it: "How am I going to kill Muskrat?"

"Suppose you do this," it said.
"There's a round rock there,
where he lays his victims down.
So, put that rock somewhere nearby,
crawl into the lodge,
and hide yourself where the smokehole rafters come together.
Now, since he'll be paying heed entirely to someone else,
to his victim,
he's not going to see you there.
When he snatches up a man,
and jumps out of the smokehole
with his victim in his arms,
you must spring out and grab him as he lays the victim down.
Throw him over your back,
take him to where you left the round rock,
and smash him with it.
Then, carry him off to his house."

"I'll do it!" said Coyote.
"That bunch of dry grass
is surely one who always gives me good advice!"

He put the grass back where it came from,
and plugged it up with the gopher's head.
Then, he went back down and put the rock in another place.
He crawled into the lodge,
and hid where the rafters came together.

The men arrived, carrying deer meat.
They handed it down through the smokehole
until they had passed it all in.
Then, they crawled in themselves,
one after the other,
until everyone was in.
The very last one scooted in on his bottom.

Just at that moment,
Muskrat jumped up, tapping and clattering,
carried him off and laid him down.
He made him scream—
he made him sound terrified.

Coyote, moving up behind Muskrat,
sprang to where he was,
and, feeling around with his paws, asked:
"Where, oh where is my round rock?"
Then, Coyote grabbed Muskrat,
carried him off somewhere,
and smashed him with the rock.
And, when he had put the corpse on his back,
he carried it in his arms to Muskrat's house,
and laid it on the ground outside.

Muskrat's wife rushed out.
She was just picking up the corpse
when she saw that it was her husband,
and she dropped it.

Coyote made a lunge for her,
grabbed her, and laid her down.
He almost thrust into her, but she said:
"Ouch! You're squeezing me! Raise yourself up a little!"

He raised himself up,
and she dived over into her underwater lodge.

When he had dived in after her,
and had chased her all around under the water,
he crawled out, cursing himself.

Wringing out his wet rabbitskin blanket,
which was cinched up around him,
he cursed himself.
"What a bungler I am, indeed!
I, Coyote, have always been a bungler!
Why am I always so trusting?
Why couldn't I hang onto her?"
He kept on cursing himself.

Afterwards, he said to Muskrat's corpse:
"Your kind are not going to bother human beings.
And when people tell tales about you,
      they'll say:
'Coyote is the one who killed that Muskrat.'
You've been wicked,
so you'll make your home along the rivers.
That's where you'll live,
and you'll never bother people again.
That's what everyone will know,
when they tell old tales."

Then, he went back down to where the people were.
When he got there, he said:
"You all stay here now. I'm going away."

And they said: "Very well!"
And there, long ago, they stayed in that same country.

But Coyote went away.

That's the end of it.

Coyote Marries His Daughter

Once, when Old Man Coyote was wandering around in the
    North Country,
he came upon a house.
He married and settled down there.
He stayed there, spending his time hunting fieldmice.

Then he had a daughter.

He lived with his wife and did nothing but hunt fieldmice.
As time passed, and his daughter was growing bigger,
he just went on, doing ordinary things.

He had a son.

The Coyote daughter grew into a very fine woman.

Then, Coyote thought things over.
"I wonder if there isn't some way I could manage to marry this
    woman," he pondered.
"What if I should be sick?
Then, I'll lie down and, after a bit, I'll seem to be dying.
If I tell them I'm dying, they'll take it as a fact."

So he went off hunting and came home at dusk.
After a while, when he had been lying down, he spoke.
"I was so sick I almost didn't make it back," he said.

He didn't sleep much that night.
At sunup, he just kept lying there.
"I think I'm very sick," he said.

His wife and daughter went out to gather food from time to
    time.
"Just pick up anything you can find to eat
so that you can keep your two children alive,"
he told his wife.

"I'm very sick, but I'll get well.
I wonder what I'll do.
Maybe I won't get well.
But all of you stay here," he said to them.

"Over yonder there lives a certain man who looks like me.
Later, when your daughter marries him,
take whatever her husband gives you
and make a life with him.
When I die, that's what you must do."
Coyote just lay there.
"Perhaps the house may burn down some time,"
        he said.
"After you have seen my remains, go away."

Later, when the others had gone gathering,
Coyote got some deer bones together,
put them in the house, and set fire to it.
It looked as if it had burned down by accident.
The others came back and saw only charred bones
left in the place where he had been lying.

The next morning, after they had mourned for him,
they went to the place he had told them to go.
They found the house, and stayed there.

Coyote had disguised himself
by smearing his fur with pine-pitch
so that, when the others got there, he married that woman.
His mother-in-law and brother-in-law moved in
and they all lived together.

Then the brothers-in-law took to hunting fieldmice.
And once, when Coyote was digging,
the coating of pitch fell out of his armpit.
His brother-in-law saw it.
They came home when it was getting dark.

The next day, when Coyote went hunting,
his son stayed home and spoke to his mother.

"Oh, mother! He does just like my father!
And he looks like him!
He goes about things the same way!
The stuff he smeared on himself has come out of his armpit!
I saw it! I'm sure he's my father!"

So the mother and daughter packed everything up
and they all left in a rage.

Coyote came back to find the place deserted.
Bewildered, he looked all around; then he went away.

"I'm really a wicked one!" he said to himself.
"When they are telling stories, people will say:
'Coyote married his own daughter, long ago.' "

He walked off along the edge of the forest.

Coyote and Frog Old Woman

Once, Old Man Coyote came to the North Country.
He married Frog Old Woman and they lived there.

They were invited to a dance.
"I hear there's going to be a dance,"
said the boy who brought the message.
"They say there'll be a singing contest, too.
Good singers from all around have been asked to come.
I hear it will be a big celebration."

"Good," said Coyote. "I'm going to go and sing."

When the sun had come up six times,
he jumped out of the house.
But his wife had been sick for two days.
She just lay there.

"What are you doing?" asked Coyote.
"Aren't you going to watch the dance?
Are you all worn out?"

"Yes," said Frog Old Woman.
"Why don't you go on by yourself?
I'll just lie here. I'm too weak to be up and around."

So, tossing some firewood into the house for her,
Coyote took off.

But when he got there, the singers were singing.
Brush Crane was singing,
Bluejay was singing,
Antelope was singing,
Little White Root was singing,
and, as Coyote arrived,
Tadpole was singing,

Shitepoke was singing,
and Kingfisher was singing.
All of them were singing.

After Coyote got there, he sang.
They were having the singing contest.
The women danced. Wolf sang.
Very fine looking women danced.

Now, among them was one spectacularly beautiful woman.
Coyote started dancing and,
when he had gone around a few times,
he grabbed her and carried her off down the hill.
He threw her down in a dark place
and stuck it into her.

"There are so many women around here!
Do you really like the looks of me?" she asked.
It turned out that she was Frog Old Woman, his wife.

He flew into a rage,
and beat her up and rolled her all around.
Then he went back up to the dance.

Just as he got back to the dance,
there happened to be a completely different woman
who was also very beautiful.

He went back to see if his wife was still where he had left her.
"I'll just go have a look," he said.
He rushed back and, when he had nearly got there,
he tiptoed up and peeked at her secretly through the bushes.
She was still flopped down where he had left her.
He sneaked away and went back to the dance.

After he got back, he stood around a little while;
then he started dancing with that beautiful woman.
When they had gone around in the dance a few times,
he clutched her to himself and ran off down the hill again.

He threw her down in a dark place
and lay down between her legs.

"Am I the only good-looking one?" she asked.
It turned out that she was the old woman, his wife.

He kicked her all around, whacked her with a club,
and left her lying there while he went back up to the dance.

And there that very same beautiful woman was dancing!
It was Frog Old Woman!
She knew what Coyote was like
and she didn't want to see nice women bothered by him.
So, she got the best of Coyote, after all.

The singing contest went on till daybreak.
Nobody liked Tadpole Man's song,
so Tadpole Man got angry and stole all the songs.
Then no one could sing since they couldn't remember the
     songs,
so they all stopped the contest.

When they were telling the old stories, the people used to say:
"In olden days, the creatures used to have singing contests.
So now, when people are going to sing,
they'll sing the ancient songs.
If someone knows a song,
the others will want to hear it.
They'll tell him to sing it and he'll sing it.
They'll know the songs, women along with men,
and they'll sing them.
All the people everywhere will sing these songs.

Coyote had done badly for himself.
He lost the contest and left.
When he got home, he told his wife:
"I didn't see the singing and dancing.
I was sitting around
smoking tobacco with the other elders till dawn."

Now, Bluejay had gotten ready for the dance
by decking himself out with feathers.
He used his grandmother's pubic hair to dress up with.
When it got dark and he began to sing,
the women hollered out:
"Bluejay says he's decked himself out
in his grandmother's pubic hair!"
He was so ashamed that he stayed only a little while,
and then he went away.

In the morning, they all left, one after another.
They trudged off in all directions,
kicking up the dust.
And then it must have been that the land was silent.

Coyote's Adventures

Once, a long time ago, Old Man Coyote got married.
He had two wives and a mother-in-law living with him.

One day, he went out hunting.
When he came back home, he said to the women:
"I hear that the Piss-ant Orphans are going out to hunt deer!"

"Is that so?" answered his mother-in-law.

"They've asked me to go along," said Coyote.
"If you would all like to go with me,
we'll all leave in the morning."
So then they went to sleep.

The next morning, Coyote said:
"We'd better get started.
Those Piss-ants might just go away and leave us, you know."
So as soon as the women had everything packed up, they went.

They went along for awhile until they came to a river.
"Wade on in, everybody," said Coyote.
"This river is the one that people call 'Slippery River.' "
So the women waded in.

"The river's pretty deep. I think you'd better hold your skirt up,"
said Coyote to his mother-in-law.

As she was crossing over, he got right up close behind her.
By and by he nudged her in the ass
and shoved it all the way in between her thighs.
"Hnn, hnn," she said. "The fish must be bumping into me!"

"That's the way they do in Slippery River," said Coyote.
All the way across, he kept messing around like that.
He only stopped when they were wading out on the other side.

So then they got across and went along on their way.
And, after they had come a little distance, they made camp.

Coyote said: "Stay here while I go take a look ahead.
Maybe those Piss-ants live right around here somewhere."
And he left.

When he got a little ways off, he said:
"Rain, fall down on this place!
Come tonight, rain!"
Then he nosed all around and about
until he found a deer that some cougar had killed a few days
       before.
He cut off a piece and carried it back with him to camp.

Along about dusk, just as he arrived,
it began to cloud over.

Coyote said to the women:
"It seems to me that the rain is saying: 'I'm going to fall!' "

And then Coyote built a bark hut.
He built it strong on one side,
but, on the other side where he was going to be sleeping,
he made it flimsy.

His two wives roasted the deer meat—
which did, in fact, stink a little—
and they all fell to.
"Anything those Piss-ant Orphans kill always stinks,
but then, let's just eat it anyway," said Coyote.

Just as they were settling down for the night, it started to rain.
But the women went to sleep just the same.

Coyote, though, jumped up and said:
"I'm getting very wet. I think I'll sleep over here."
And he crawled over to where his mother-in-law's feet were
       sticking out.

"I'll just put this right down here," he said,
putting a piece of bark on edge between himself and his wives.
"I might just touch one of you."

The women were all asleep, the old woman too.
Coyote crawled over and lay on top of her.
He kept fucking her until it was almost daylight,
but, just before dawn, he jumped up and ran away.,

When the old woman woke up, she gave birth to a litter of kids.
Then she bound them in cradleboards and started off,
carrying them on her back.

She went along, and, when she came to Slippery River,
she waded across and kept on going till she got back home.
She clambered up, stood over the smokehole, and hollered:
"Is Coyote in there?"

Now, Coyote *was* there. But he whispered to the others:
"Say 'No. He isn't.' "

But somebody said: "Yes. He's here!"

Then the old woman said: "Coyote! Here are your whelps!
You can have them!"

Coyote popped up out of the smokehole and ran away.
She threw his kids along after him, but he got safely away.

He crawled in somewhere and stayed there. He said to
          himself:
"Some day, people will call me 'bad Coyote.'
They'll say:
'Once upon a time, long ago, he knocked up his mother-in-
          law!' "

When he was sure all was safe,
he crawled out of his hiding place
and ambled along until he came down into the country
          hereabouts.

He sat down on a log right alongside a little hut
and sprawled out.

Someone spoke to him.
"You there! You look like a *yomím,* flopped out there on that
   log!
You'd better come and do some curing for me!"

"Is it possible she could be talking to *me*?" said Coyote.
"Maybe I'll just get up and hop along this log."
So he stood up and hopped along the log.

The old woman said: "You, hopping along that log there!
I'm talking to *you*!"

"She seems to be talking to me, all right," said Coyote.
He jumped down off the log.

"You who jumped down! I'm talking to *you*!"

"Yes! She *is* talking to me!" exclaimed Coyote.
He went over to where she was and sat down.

Then, she spoke.
"My daughter is sick. If you can do it, I'm asking you to cure
   her."

Coyote said:
"I just go along just being myself,
talking the way I always talk.
I can cure people!
I've travelled all around,
even in the land of the Clam-eaters.
Now, I've gotten down here,
a long way from home.
Everything I do and say makes people get well,
even though I'm not really trying to cure people."

The old woman's daughter was in the hut.
Coyote scooted along on his butt into the hut

and sat down beside her.
He started singing.
"When a spirit speaks to me,
it speaks like this:
'Being loath to do battle,
I have always talked through you.
I am the one who raps the spirit-post.
If everyone closes up the house
and makes it tight and strong,
then I will speak through the *yomím*.
If the people will crawl outside
then I, myself, the spirit,
will speak through the *yomím*.' "

So, the old woman crawled out,
sealed up the hut and stayed outside.

Meanwhile, Coyote was singing.
it sounded loud and fast.

The old woman said:
"Now he must be curing her!
He's fetched up a spirit of the dead with his doctoring!"

There was a scary sound of heavy breathing.
The old woman peeked through a cranny
and saw that Coyote was lying on top of the girl,
going at it hard and strong.

In a fury, the old woman grabbed up a big stick
and sprang inside the hut.
Just as she was about to hit him,
Coyote jumped up and,
breaking off his cock,
bolted out of the smokehole and ran away.
He dashed off to Badger's house and stayed there.

Now, the girl got sicker,
and the old woman went to Badger's house
and asked him to cure her.

She said:
"I got Old Man Coyote to agree to cure my daughter.
When he was getting ready to start, he ordered me out of the
     house.
While I was waiting outside,
I heard him singing and gasping for breath,
so I peeked in and saw him lying on top of the girl.
That's why he was gasping!
When I sprang in there, ready to give him a whack,
he jumped and bolted
and broke off his dingus inside my daughter.
Now, I want you to come and doctor her
so that she can get rid of that thing!"

Coyote was there with them,
but he had disguised himself.
He spoke, then, and said to Badger:
"A little while back, that Coyote did something like that to *me*.
Are you going to doctor her yourself and draw out the pain?
If you use all your power,
and, if the spirits make you brave,
then the girl will get strong and well.
I'll go along with you."

So they went.
When Badger had painted white stripes on his forehead,
they set out for the old woman's hut.

After they got there, Badger started his song.
He sang for awhile; then he said:
"When I have drawn the pain out,
what will you do with it?"

"I'm going to put it into the fire," said the old woman.

But Coyote said:
"It has always been that if anyone puts a pain into the ashes of
     the fire,
it just swims away.
Therefore, it would be better to throw the pain into the water."

But the old woman said: "I'll put it in the fire!"

After singing and singing,
Badger finally drew out Coyote's pisser
and laid it on the ground.
The old woman opened a place in the ashes
and got ready to roast it.

But, just then, Coyote began to make magic.
"May melting ice rise up from underground!"
It was Coyote who said it.

When the old woman had a place open in the ashes,
she laid the cock down on the cold ground
and got ready to put it into the fire.
Just as she picked it up,
Coyote grabbed it away from her,
clutched it to himself, sprang out of the hut
and quickly ran away.

The old woman said:
"I easily guessed who Coyote was the first time,
but the second time, I just didn't recognize him."

Later on, Badger went his ways.
And ever after, he painted stripes on his face
whenever he set out to cure someone.

But Coyote went along until he saw a place where a whole lot
        of women were staying.
When he was still a little way off from there,
he made magic again:
"Let some old kind of pack-basket appear,
and a sifting tray, and also a worn-out cradleboard."
And the things appeared.

He mashed up a *lókbom* root.
When it was all pounded and mashed up fine,
he shaped it into a woman's what-you-may-call-it
and attached it to himself.

He made a woman's bark skirt—
an old and frazzled one—
one that wouldn't cover him completely.
Then he bound his pisser into the cradleboard
and shoved it into the pack-basket.
He picked up the basket, took a staff,
and, walking all bent over the way very old people do,
he went down among the women.
Just at dusk, he came to where they were.

"Well, now," said one of the women,
"I think I see a very old woman coming along."
She took a careful look at the child.
"That doesn't look much like a child," she said.

"I'm so weak that when I took him out of the cradle
I dropped him and he hit the ground with a bump.
That's why he's so swollen up that he doesn't look like himself,"
　　said Coyote.
"It makes me feel so sad when he calls for his father."

"Ylbyl, ylbyl, ylbyl," said the child.

"That's the way he calls," said Coyote,
"and it makes me feel so sad!"
Coyote was talking like a woman.
"I'm so pitiful, sad and weak that I let him hit with a bump."

Now, though his what-you-may-call-it was covered by the bark
　　apron,
the women could see through the raggedy holes.
They all took a peek.

"How un-childlike that child looks!"
said two of the women who were in the back.
"No, it certainly is a child," said another one.
"She says it got a bump on the head.
That's why it looks so swollen."

"That thing there has the head of a pisser!"
        said the two women.
"That's why bumping swells it up like that!"

Just those two women were wary.
All the others believed Coyote.
"Look at her," they said.
"She looks just like an old woman.
Don't you see? Her thing-a-ma-jig looks just like it should!"

"Maybe so," the two women said.
They all had supper.

After darkness fell, the forest was frightening.
The women told Coyote:
"You'd better sleep here, between us.
You might get cold."
So they put him in between a couple of them
and everyone went to sleep close by—
everyone but the two women who were wary.

Then, in the dark, Coyote took out his magic sleeping powder.
He sprinkled it all around, over the women,
casting them into deeper slumber.
Then he threw off his disguise and thrust into the women—
all but the two suspicious ones.
He kept at it through the night;
then, just before dawn, he sneaked away.

What noisy, crying litters of children the women had next
        morning!

But Coyote got away.
He went down along the river for a while.
There he spied some waterbug women swimming.
It looked exciting.
He watched them secretly from behind the reeds
as they crawled out onto the river bank
and jumped back into the water again.

Wow! What an ass! Look at that one! And that one, too!"
said Coyote as he made a lunge for the fattest one.
Just as she suddenly jumped up,
he sprang sideways and grabbed her.
They went at it for a long time;
then he crawled off her and went away.

As he went along
somewhere in the middle of the world,
his pisser hurt him.

He scratched and scratched it.
At last, he cut it off, up toward the tip.
He threw the piece away and set out again.

A little further on,
it began to hurt him very much.
He cut off another piece.

Still further along, it hurt worse than ever!

He cut off the rest of it, right down to the base,
and, when he set out again,
he tumbled down and died.

He lay there, dead.

As he lay there,
two Crow brothers flew down and pecked out his eye.
Then, they started on his other eye,
but, when they tugged at it,
he came back to life and sprang up.

"As I slept,
it seemed that many *yomím* were haranguing one another,"
        said Coyote.
"That's why you two are the way you are!"

He grabbed up a stick,
threw it at them and missed.

Then he got up and went away.

He went along,
and, by and by, he came to a place in the forest
where Hummingbird was flying up to the top of a tree,
swooping down halfway to the ground,
and then gliding upwards again.
He did that many times
while Coyote stood and watched him in wonder.

Coyote said:
"Wow! You are so good at that, cousin!
If I only knew how to do that,
all the women everywhere would admire me!
Please teach me how to do it. You do it so well!"

"All right," said Hummingbird.
"If you really want to learn how, I'll teach you.
I can do it because I'm not afraid.
I just keep zooming up to the top of the tree.
Then I get out on the largest limb,
take a look over and down,
and jump."

"So that's it," said Coyote.
"I can do that.
People everywhere will be amazed
and women will say: 'He knows how to do it!' "

Then, Coyote crawled up the tree until he got to the very top.
Then he stood up.
He jumped and, when he got halfway to the bottom,
he put his nose in the air and howled like mad.
Just at that moment, he hit the ground.
He dragged and pulled himself around for a little while;
then he died.

Hummingbird left him lying there and went away.

After a while, the two Crow boys flew down
and pecked out his eye.
They were going to pluck out the other eye,
but, when they tugged at it,
Coyote woke up and sprang to his feet.

"Important men are haranguing one another as they sleep.
That's why you two are the way you are," said Coyote.

He set out again and kept going along
until he came to a place where a man lived with his wife.
And Coyote stayed with them awhile.

By and by, Coyote asked the man:
"Where did you find such a beautiful wife?
Where do good-looking women like that come from?"

"All I did was to marry a very old woman,
and, after she had lived with me for a while,
she became young and beautiful," said the man.

"So that's it," said Coyote.
"Tell me now, where do such very old women live?"

"There are quite a few houses over that way,
not too far from here," said the man.
"If you just go that way, you'll come to them.
Further on, a little beyond them,
you'll come to another house.
When you get there, you'll find an ugly old woman living there.
She's the one you want to marry.
She'll be hardly able to walk,
so pack her on your back and carry her.
After you've fetched her back here,
wait a little while.
One morning, just at daybreak,
she'll wake up as a very good-looking young woman.
That's what she'll do, and you'll be a happily married man."

"Right!" said Coyote. And he set out the next morning.

He went on past the cluster of houses
and came over the ridge to the little hut.
He crawled inside
and found an ugly old woman sprawled out on the ground.
He sat down and waited until nightfall,
then he crawled over and slept beside her.

When they woke up the next morning,
he took her by the hand and led her off.
When they had gone a little way along, she got tired,
so he hoisted her up on his back and carried her.
They got back to the man's house about dusk and went to
        sleep.
The next morning, they stayed there.

Meanwhile, the man went out hunting.
He came back in the evening, carrying a deer he had killed.

"How in the world did you manage to kill that deer?"
Coyote asked.
"Tell me, and let me go hunting now, too."

"Well," said the man,
"I just went around to where a deer trail winds up behind this
        mountain
and sat down there.
Then, I picked up a heavy club and smashed them.
I stood alongside the trail and clubbed them to death."

"Well, I'm going to do the same thing," said Coyote.

He set out the next morning,
and went along until he came to the place the man had told
        him about.
The trail was, in fact, a big one, made by bears—
one that they went along to get to their feeding grounds.
Coyote took up his post alongside the trail.

Then the bears came.
They rushed over the ridge
and kept coming and coming,
going past him as he shouted:
"You're not the one I want!
I'm looking for a big one!"

Now, as they were going past,
a really big one did come along.
Just as he came over the ridge,
Coyote let him have it, but the club bounced off with a clang.
He hit him, but he didn't kill him.

Then the bear lunged at Coyote
and hugged him to death with his forepaws.

When Coyote hadn't come back home by sunup,
the man went over and killed the old woman,
who was actually his grandmother.
He picked her body up and threw it into a pond.

But the next morning the old woman came back to life again,
and went home to live in her hut.

All this time, Coyote was dead.
The two Crow brothers came to where he was lying
and pecked out his eye.

But, when they started tugging at the other eye,
he sprang up.

"Perhaps important men are shouting at one another," he said.
"That's why you are the way you are!"

Then he got up and went away.

As he went along,
he heard something like two women singing a little way off.

It sounded very fine. He stood listening.
The singing seemed to be coming from close behind a nearby
    ridge.

"Well, now!" he pondered. "I wonder if they see me."

They sang in time with him as he was stepping along.

"They *must* see me," he said.

He lengthened his stride,
stepping out to the rhythm of the women's song.
He went along like that, keeping in step.

At the same time,
they sounded as if they were nearby watching *him.*
The sound came from over the ridge.

He hurried up to the top of the slope and looked all around.
The sound seemed to be coming from the next ridge.
He jumped up and ran across the valley and up the other
        slope.
When he took another look around,
they sounded as if they were still further away.

Coyote called out to them.
"You must be really smitten with me
since you admire me so much," he said.
"I'll get to where you are,
and, when I do, you can have a good look at me!"

He jumped up and loped along until he got tired.
Then he stopped at dusk and made camp.
Although these two women were singing far away,
they sounded as if they were right there where he was.
When morning came, he couldn't hear them singing any more.

Now he had just set out again
when he came to the house where Cottontail lived.
And Cottontail told him:

"There are some women who have dances,
but I don't go to watch them."

"Well, then," said Coyote, "let's the two of us go dance."

"All right. We'll go when it gets dark," said Cottontail.

After nightfall, the dancing and singing sounded wonderful.
So the two of them went.

When they had gone on a little way, Coyote said:
"Stop right where you are! I'll tell you what.
You'd better wait here."

"All right," said Cottontail.

"And keep this here with you," said Coyote, handing him his
　　　cock.
"Women are very wary of me when I'm wearing it.
If these women go for me, I'll whistle.
When you hear me, come and bring it with you."

So, Cottontail stayed back
while Coyote went on to where the women were dancing and
　　　hollering.
They sounded fine.
As he got there,
he could see that there were some good-looking women
　　　dancing.
Two really beautiful ones took that Coyote fellow
and led him away.
He went along with them,
and they all wandered off, holding hands.

When they got to where Coyote had left Cottontail,
they all sat down.

Coyote whistled.
The place was deserted.
He whistled again.

"What's the matter with you?" asked one of the women.

"I'm just kidding around," said Coyote.
"I must say, it makes me feel fine,
going around with two women like you.
It makes me feel wonderful!"

The women laughed,
threw their legs across him and hugged and kissed him.
It was a sight to behold!

"Wooeeee," said Coyote.
"Wait right here, you two!"

He ran up to where he'd left Cottontail,
and, when he got there, he whistled.
He didn't hear anything.
He was really angry.
He searched all around but he saw no sign of Cottontail,
so he went back to where he had left the women.

"What are you looking for?" they asked.

Oh, nothing," said Coyote.
"I was just fooling around."

Then they all lay down,
and the two women put him in the middle,
hugging him and tickling him.

He jumped up again and scouted around,
going over the same old ground,
but he still saw no one.
He was very, very angry.

Now, when Coyote had left Cottontail to go to the dance,
a couple of Star Women came and led Cottontail away.
By and by, Cottontail fucked the woman who was a little older.
He made her gasp until she cried out.

The younger woman said:
"How can a fellow like that make you almost cry out?
No little pipsqueak could do that to me!"
So he fucked *her* and made *her* cry out.
She was gasping so hard it sounded really frightening.

Meanwhile,
Coyote bedded down with the other women until daybreak.
Then he left them and went to Cottontail's house.
Cottontail was there.
Coyote rushed up and glared at him in a rage.

"I just feel like I want to kill you," he said.
"What did you do with that thing I left with you?"
He was furious.

"Two women came and led me away by the hand," said
        Cottontail.

"And then what?" demanded Coyote.

"I just went ahead and fucked them with your thing,"
        said Cottontail.

"Oho!" said Coyote.
"I really made those two women cry," said Cottontail.

"Mm *hmm*!" said Coyote.
"That thing *will* make little women cry!"

He felt very much as if *he'd* been fucking.
He quickly got over being angry.
When Cottontail handed it back to him,
he washed it in the creek and put it away.
"This thing is a good one," he said.
"It's more than enough, even for big women."

He didn't dance that day,
but he stayed the night
and, the next morning, feeling good,
he set off down the trail.

Tales of
Other
Beings

Fisher and Woodrat

Long ago, in olden times,
Fisher and some Cottontail boys built a house
and lived in it.

Now, Fisher said to the Cottontails:
"Stay in the house, all of you. You must stay here.
I'm going away,
but you must all stay safely here.
Don't go anywhere!
I'm going off yonder in the morning!"
And, in the morning, he went.
But that whole bunch of Cottontail boys stayed there.

Before he left, he told them when he would return.
"In a few days—about six days—I'll be back,
unless someone does me in on the trail," he said.
"But you must all stay safely here."
And they stayed.

The next morning, just at dawn,
one of the boys crawled out of the house.
He sat there for a while until he was fully awake;
then he flopped down on top of the smokehole.

Now, just across the way,
Woodrat lived with his grandmother
in a sweat lodge which he had built.
Pretty soon, Woodrat crawled out and said:
"How's everything?"
It was Woodrat who spoke.

"Old Woodrat makes me puke!" said the Cottontail.
"Shitting on his grandmother's blankets—
stinking everything up—
shitting all over the house—
pissing on everything—

yucky old Woodrat!
Makes his whole house stink!"

"Hahm! Hahm!" said Woodrat.
Grandmother! Fetch me my net!
He's making fun of me!"

And she brought it out.
And he crossed over and threw the net over the smokehole,
and then he stamped on the top of the house.
He kept stamping until one of the Cottontails sprang out,
and, just as he did, he got caught in the net.

Then Woodrat grabbed the Cottontail boy up
and carried him back home in his arms.
And, when he had carried him in and let him go,
the grandmother grabbed him, skinned him,
cut him up and roasted him,
and the two of them had him for supper.

The next morning, Woodrat crawled out and said: "Hey!"

One of the Cottontails stuck his head out of the smokehole.
"Vomity old Woodrat!" he said.
"Shitting on his grandmother,
pissing on everything—
a pukey old Woodrat, stinking things up!"
Then he popped back into the house.

Then, Woodrat said: "Hahm! Hahm!
He said nasty things to me!
Grandmother! Bring out my net!"

He crossed over, stretched it over the door,
and stamped on the house. He kept stamping.

One of the Cottontails jumped out
and got caught in the net.

Woodrat grabbed him up, carried him across,
and gave him to his grandmother.
She skinned him out and they had him for supper.

And, the next morning, again,
Woodrat crawled outside and said: "Halloo!"

One of the Cottontail lads peeked out of the house.
"Bad old Woodrat!" he said.
"Shitting on his grandmother's clothes—
making everybody want to throw up—
pissing all over the house—
what a revolting, stinking Woodrat!"

So then, "Hahm! Hahm! Hahm!" said Woodrat.
"He says such terrible things to me!
Fetch me out my net, Grandmother!"

And she gave it to him.

He went across to the other house
and stretched it over the door.
Then he stamped and stamped on the roof.

In a little while, the Cottontail sprang out,
and Woodrat caught him in the net.
Then he grabbed him up and carried him home.

And so, there was only one of the Cottontails left.
He crawled back behind the fireplace in Fisher's house,
and stayed there.

When Woodrat got home with the one he had caught,
he and his grandmother skinned him
and roasted him for their evening meal.

Then the next day, Woodrat crawled out and said "Halloo!"
But this time, no one poked his head out,
and Woodrat said: "There aren't any more!
I've killed them all!"

And again the next day, he stuck his head out and said:
    "Halloo!"
And again, no one peeked out of Fisher's house.

"Grandmother," he exclaimed,
"I do believe I've killed them all!
I don't see any of them! Nobody's crawling out!"

The next morning, he took a look again.
"Halloo!" he said. But no one appeared.
"I do believe I must have done in every last one of them!"

Now, just at dusk, Fisher arrived home.
He crawled into the house.
There seemed to be no one there.
But then, in a moment,
one of the boys crawled up from behind the fireplace.
He spoke:
"Woodrat came over here after us.
He stamped on the house;
the others sprang out, one by one,
and he killed them.
He was out to kill us all,
but I didn't jump out!
I was frightened, I stayed still, and I survived!"

"Oho!" said Fisher.
And in the morning he set out to get Woodrat.
He went across to the other house,
and, when he got there, he crawled inside,
and killed both grandson and grandmother.
And he spoke.
"Telling tales, people will say:
'You're nothing but a woodrat.
Nobody pays any attention to you.
You run around among the tumbled rocks
and do nothing bad to anybody.' "

And, after that, he crossed over,
and, when he got back to his own house,

he stayed there.
"Well," he said to Cottontail,
"little brother, just go on living in a place like this,
staying hidden under the bushes.
I, myself, will be one who roams far and wide,
but you will be one who doesn't travel around much—
one who stays right around here."
It was Fisher who spoke.

And then he set out.
"All right," he said, "I'm going! Stay here!"
And he went.

Cottontail, flicking his ears, watched him go;
then he, too, went away from there.

That's all, they say.

Nighthawk

Nighthawk built himself a sweat lodge
and moved into it.

And about the same time,
another man also built a sweatlodge,
just across the way,
and moved into it.
And that man killed a lot of deer.
People heard about it,
and, when they were gossiping among themselves,
one of them told the others:
"They tell me that fellow is a regular deer-killer!"

Now, a good distance away,
a man lived with his two daughters.
"Daughters," he said to them, "you two better go down that way.
When you get down a ways, you'll see a house,
and there will be a couple of black bear hides
tied up by the smokehole.
The black bear hides will be hung up over the door.
That's the place you will go to.
But, across from there, a bad man lives.
There's nothing he won't kill!
You mustn't go there!"

"Very well," they said.
And they started off.

Now Nighthawk saw them,
and, when he had carried off the bear hides,
he tied them over his own door.
Then they hung down over the door,
and, when he had crawled into the house,
he sat there, playing the flute.

About that time, the two women got there.
"Here's the place our father told us about," said one.
So they crawled in
and sat down on either side of the flute-player.

Later, the man from across the way came home from hunting.
He crossed over to Nighthawk's house,
and took back his black bear hides.
When he got home with them,
he hung his bear hides up again.

It got dark,
and Nighthawk, across the way,
slept with those two women.

In the morning, when they woke up,
the two women crawled out,
and there, on the house across,
the two bear hides were tied up.
There they were, hanging on the other house.

When they both saw this,
the older sister said:
"Which place, I wonder, were we really supposed to come to?"

Then the younger sister spoke.
"I think we were supposed to go over there,
but we seem to have come to another place!
So, where should we go?" she asked.
"Are we just going to stay here?"

They stood around a while; then the older sister said:
"Let's go where we *should* go!"

Then they went across.

"That man stole these things
and hung them up on his house,"

said one of the women as they talked together.
"*That* must have been what got us to go there!
So, let's go into *this* house and sit down!"

"Let's do that!" said the other.
So they crawled in and sat down,
side by side, in the hunter's house.

After a little while, someone seemed to be singing.
And as he sang, the wind began to blow.
He sang, and the wind blew harder.
It started to rain, and still he sang.
It rained harder and harder.
The next morning, still he sang.

It rained and rained.
The river rose, and still it rained.
The water pounded down on the roof of the lodge.

His singing got louder and stronger.

The water began to leak into the house,
and still he sang.

Then all the hunter's kinswomen got up
and crossed over to Nighthawk's house.
And, when they had crawled in,
they bashed in his head with a club.
For it was Nighthawk that was singing.

They spoke.
"People will say:
'Long ago, that evil Nighthawk got angry with some women,
and he made a flood come with his singing.'
From now on, you'll have nothing to do with humans.
You will just be a nighthawk,
a bird, who can't do anything.
But men will keep lying to women and marrying them!"

Then, after they had killed him,
everybody crossed back over to their own lodge,
and, little by little, the rain stopped,
and the skies cleared.
They all crawled into their houses.

There they lived, in those old days, long ago.

That's the end of it.

Mountain Lion and His Children

Mountain Lion went deer-hunting.
When he had packed some food on his back, he went,
and after he had gone quite a ways along,
he set up his camp for the night.
He slept, and, in the morning, he awoke and ate.
Then he strung his bow and went off to hunt.
After hunting all around a while, he shot a deer,
and, along toward dark, he carried it back to camp.
He gutted the deer, cut it into pieces and hung it up.
In the morning, when the meat was somewhat dry,
he stuffed it into a bag and set out for home.
He went along until he got there.

Now, his two children, who usually came out to meet him,
were nowhere to be seen.
The place was deserted.

"What can have happened?" he asked himself.
He threw the deer meat down; then he sat on the ground
and peered into the house.
He saw that someone was lying over alongside his wife.
They were lying there together.

"I wonder where my two children could be," he thought.
He peered into the house again, but he saw nothing.
"Where, where could they be?"

He searched around, found their tracks,
and followed them down the trail.
But then he turned back again,
and, when he got to his house,
he set fire to it.
He burned the house to the ground.

Now earlier, when the two children were playing in the house,
a man crawled in and sat down.

"Your father, where has he gone?" he asked.

But they didn't answer him. They were frightened.
They jumped over behind their mother.

Then the old woman spoke.
"He's gone deer-hunting," she said.

"Good!" said the man.

He sat there cross-legged awhile,
then he crawled over and got up close beside her.

"What are you doing?" she asked.

"What am I doing!" he exclaimed.
"I'm going to make you my woman!"

"What are you talking about?
I already have a man," she said.

"Nevertheless," he said, "I'm going to make you my woman."
And he grabbed her.

"Because you and I have done like this together,
men, talking bad and stealing women,
        will say:
'It's all right! Even in olden times,
they used to do bad things to women
so that they had children!'
The women will believe them,
and, even though they already have a man,
they will take another one."

So saying, the man lay down beside her,
and the woman said nothing.

Meanwhile, the two children cowered by the fire.
Then, holding each other's hand,
they crept out of the house.
After they stood around outside for awhile,
they started off.

By and by, they came to an anthill,
tore it open with their hands,
and crawled in.

Angrily, they set off, went along for awhile,
and made camp nearby.

The sister was the younger, they say,
and her brother was a little bigger.

They had already gone
when that old man, their father,
returned from hunting and burned down the house.

Then after that, the old man searched for them.
He followed their tracks, but he couldn't find them.
He circled all around to the places where they often played,
looking for traces of them.
He went weeping and crying—every day he cried.
He searched and searched for signs of them,
but he saw nothing.
Nowhere could he find any trace of them.

He went around up there in the North Country,
looking everywhere—everywhere.
Then he went southwards, going all around.
He went east and north again,
searching for their tracks.
He circled around everywhere, throughout the land,
but he still found no trace.

He went further and further away.
"To what part of the world could they have gone
so that I cannot see their trail?" he pondered.

He went on and on—toward the sunrise.
He turned and went northwards again.
"Where, oh where could they be?
Shall I never find them?" he asked himself.
Day after day he wept, but he kept on searching.

Finally, he came back to the place he had started from.
He just sat down and stayed there, crying.
"I have wandered through many a country," he said,
drying his tears.
"I must go home again!"

So he set out for home.
He went through many different places
until he got back to his house.
Then he followed the tracks
which the children had made long before.
He went along.
A little way from the house,
in a solitary place, the tracks suddenly stopped.

He didn't know how that could be.
"What am I to do?" he wondered.
After he had stood there for awhile,
he took a look around and spied the anthill.
He scraped away the sand,
and there he saw a hole going down and down.
He crawled into it.

Now, there, nearby,
was the place where the children had made camp.
He saw their tracks going away from there.
He stayed the night in that same place.
In the morning, he got up and set out again.
He went along until he came to their next campsite,
a little further on.

When his sister grew tired,
the boy had picked her up on his back, it seemed.
And, after he had carried her a little ways,

he had put her down again.
They had kept on doing that,
getting a little distance,
then stopping again for the night.

From their tracks, Mountain Lion saw what they had done.
He saw their camping place as he went along
and, a little beyond,
he, himself, spent the night.

The children had killed some birds and eaten them.
By the time they had gotten that far,
they had grown a little bigger.

It looked as if they had gone on and on,
and, a little further on, again they made camp.
There they had dug up camas bulbs
and made an evening meal of them.

Mountain Lion came to that place
and continued on his way.

And again, a little further along,
he came to their camping place.
And, when that old man got there,
he himself spent the night.

At a place further on,
the children had shot some ducks.
They had dug camas, and all kinds of things to eat,
and they had made their evening meal.
When the old man got there,
he saw what they had done,
and, when he had eaten that same kind of food,
he slept.
In the morning, he ate again and went on his way.

Going on like that, the old man ate what there was to eat.
He kept going, always camping where they had camped.

After he had travelled a far distance,
he came to one of their camping places.
they had killed a fawn there.
They had made a bow.
They had left the bow behind, along with a little seed-beater.
They gathered seeds with it, and then left it behind.
And then, they had gone on their way.

The old man came to that same place and stayed there.
He took down the deer, which was hanging up,
and roasted it. He cooked some camas in the ashes.
He ate.
In the morning, when he woke up,
he ate some more of the roasted deer meat and the camas.

Then he went, and he travelled along,
and, again, he came to a place where the children had stayed.
And *there* a *big* deer was hanging up.
A gathering basket, a digging stick and a big bow were left
        behind.
Well-made things were left behind.

When he got there,
he roasted meat from the deer,
he baked some camas,
and, raking it out with the gathering basket,
he served it up and,
when all was well prepared,
he ate his evening meal.
And in the morning, when he woke up,
he did the same thing again.
He roasted some deer meat,
baked some camas,
prepared everything nicely
and served it out on a willow platter.
When he had eaten, he went away.

After he had gone along for a while,
it seemed as if he might be about to catch up with the children.

He went along until he came to another of their camping
      places.
There, they had shot a brown bear, gutted it and hung it up.
They had nicely prepared the bear skin
and had left all this behind.
And they left behind a little burden basket,
and a willow tray,
and also some camas which they had dug.

When the old man had gotten there,
he thought: "Now I'm really about to catch up with them!"

He took down some of the bear meat which was hanging there,
and he roasted it and ate his evening meal.
Then, when he had slept, he got up and ate again.
And, afterwards, he went on his way.

Now, when the children had gone on,
they had left a little hut behind.
They had covered it over with bark and brush
and had camped there for the night.

Mountain Lion arrived there.

A burden basket and a sifting tray were left behind.
There was a quiver hanging there.
Deer meat was hanging up.
Bear meat was hanging up.

When he got there, he built a fire.
He took down some of the deer meat and roasted it
and ate it.
Then he slept,
and, in the morning, when he woke up,
he roasted some more of the deer meat
and ate it.
Then he went on his way.

He travelled and travelled
until he came to yet another place where they had camped.

And, when he got there,
he saw that there was a black bear skin hanging up.
And they had left a fisher-pelt quiver,
and a burden basket and a sifting tray.

"I think I've almost caught up with them!" he said.
And again, in the morning, when he had finished eating,
he went on his way.

Now, Mountain Lion had grown very old.
He had come so very far, travelling and travelling.
When he looked far ahead,
he saw a great winter lodge there.
He kept going along until he got there.
He was very old.

He sat down beside the lodge,
and, stretching out on the ground, he lay there.
The brother and sister looked out at that very old man.
"Who has come?" they asked.

Then the old man's daughter crawled out of the door.
"He surely looks like my father," she said.

Then her brother crawled out too.
He looked the old man over carefully,
but his father had grown so old
that his son could not quite recognize him.
He went back into the house,
brought out his bow,
and shot the old man lying there.

His father died.

Later, he picked the old man up in his arms,
and carried him down and laid him in a spring of water.

And after that, in the morning,
when the old man had become a youth again,
he came to life and rose up out of the spring.

And he went into the lodge,
and there was his daughter with her husband and children.
And when Mountain Lion came in,
they gave him food,
and when they had all eaten, they talked together.

His daughter said:
"When my brother and I saw that some strange person had
     grabbed our mother,
we became frightened and ran away."
Her brother said:
"And so, we finally got as far as this place."

So they all lived together in that country, long ago.

That is all, they say.

The Great Serpent

There was once an old man and his wife
who lived in a winter lodge
which they had built just this side of Wisótpinim.
They had a single child, a daughter,
who lived there with them.

Now, every day, along toward evening,
the girl went, without fail, to bathe in the river.
And, afterwards, she slept and dreamed.
Night after night, she dreamed a certain dream—
always the same dream.

Once, when she went to bathe,
she didn't return until dawn.
But, when it was morning,
she came up out of the river, carrying some fish,
and brought them home.
She handed them over to her father,
then she sat down and stayed there.

Later, unseen, the Great Serpent came.
From outside, he looked in through the draft-hole;
then he crawled in. He kept crawling in,
all around the sides of the room
until he filled all the space from behind the fireplace
to the other end of the lodge.
Then, with his head near the girl,
he stared fixedly into her face.
Then, when he had been there a little while,
he crawled out again.
He kept coming out and coming out
until he was all outside.
And then, he went back into the water,
crawling in and crawling in
until he disappeared.

But the young woman stayed home in the lodge.
After awhile, she spoke.
"He said: 'Come with me!' "

"Aha!" said her father.
"Tomorrow morning, I will go," she said.
"What he said to me was: 'Let's go in the morning.' "

"All right," the old man said to her.
"I suppose you'd better go."

Then, later, they went to sleep.

The next morning, the woman went to fetch water,
and she saw her lover there,
and he gave her many fish;
and she carried back the water in one hand,
and the fish in the other.

When she got back, she set the water down,
and then she handed over the fish;
and her father took them.

That same morning,
awhile after they had finished breakfast,
the Great Serpent came crawling up again.
And, just as before, he coiled himself around,
filling up all the space from behind the fireplace
to the front of the draft-hole.
And again he brought his head up beside the woman
and stared fixedly at her.

After a little while, he crawled back outside—
he kept crawling until he was all outside.
Then he crawled up the slope
and away he went toward Hanýlekim Valley.

The woman said to her father: "Now, then! I'm going!"

"Yes, yes!" he answered, "but wait!
I want to make a cane for you."
And he made her a cane,
and tied a root to the tip of it.

"When you get to your lover's lodge,
and you're standing above the smokehole,
look all around inside, then throw the root in.
Throw the root into the middle of the fireplace!

"You must say: 'If you try to molest me,
then, with that magic root,
I'll make your head throb with pain.
So, don't molest me!'
That's what you must say!"

"All right," she said, and she started off.

She caught up with her lover where he was waiting for her,
and they went on together.

He looked, then, just like a human being—
with two legs and two arms—
exactly like a human being.
They travelled along a long way together,
he and the woman.
After a while, he reached out to her
and grabbed her by the arm.

"Leave me alone!" she said.
"With this magic, mysterious thing
I might make your head throb with pain."

"Hmm!" he answered, looking away from her.

And so they kept going and going,
and, by and by, they got to his lodge.
And, when they had gotten there,
the man crawled in through the smokehole.

When he had crawled in,
the woman peeked down from above
and she flung that root down into the fire.
Then she sprang up and ran back homewards.
She kept running, and,
when she was halfway to the bank of the river,
there was a noise behind her.
It sounded like a great low rumble rolling over the land.
She took a look back.
The lodge was flying to pieces, burning.
Great flames were roiling up.
She ran.
It was, indeed, like a great clap of thunder
rolling over the land.

Paying no heed, the woman ran homeward.
She ran and ran; then she slowed to a walk and,
travelling a long way,
at last she got home again.

After she got home, she spoke to her father.
"I managed to throw it in," she said.
"When I saw that I had flung it into the midst of the fire,
I ran away.
And, after I had gotten partway home—
just to the edge of the forest—
there was a great booming noise."

"That's good," said her father.
"I gave it to you so that you could throw it just that way!"

And they all three lived there together.

Now, people say that Hanýlekim Lake
is where the Great Serpent's house was.
It caught fire and burnt down.
It fell together and the water poured in.
The Great Serpent was killed by the woman
and his house was burnt down.

And, when the Great Serpent was killed,
his house was gone forever.

That's the end of it.

The Sisters Who Married the Stars

Two women, who were just old enough to dance,
were dancing,
and, when they had stopped dancing,
at daybreak, they both went to sleep.
They slept until sometime along toward the next morning;
then they woke up and went to dig for tigerlily bulbs.
And, when the women got back at dark,
everyone was dancing around again.

After they had danced round and round,
they danced, stepping forward and back.
Then, just as the daylight came down over the rim of the hills,
when everyone had chased the singers away,
the two women went to sleep again.

Then, in a little while, one of them dreamed.

Their mother said: "If you dream something bad,
then, when you have pierced your earlobes,
you must dive into the water.
Afterwards,
you must blow all the bad things away from yourselves.
Then sleep will heal you,
and you will wake up feeling well."

Now, when those two women dreamed,
they dreamed of Star Beings,
and they did *not* blow the dream away!
They did *not* pierce their ears!
They did *not* bathe in the stream!

And, when the dance was done,
they went with their mother to the spring,
planning to stay there and dig for tigerlily bulbs.

And, when they got there, they made camp.
They lay down there to go to sleep,
and, as they lay on their backs and stared up into the sky,
they talked with each other.

One of them asked the other:
"Would you like to go up there?
If I could just get up there,
I would like to have a look at that very red, bright star!"

"I feel the same way," said the other.
"I would like to get up to that star that looks bluish!
I wonder what he looks like!"

Then, those two went to sleep,
and, when they woke up in the morning,
they found themselves with the Star Beings in the sky.

That old woman, their mother,
who was left behind down here,
went searching for them.
She sought to find out where they might have gone.
She tried to find their footprints,
but could not see them anywhere.
Since she could find no footprints to follow,
she trudged along back home, weeping.

When she got back, the people came home from hunting.
They kept coming, and, when they arrived,
they, too, searched for the daughters.
They looked and looked for tracks,
but, when they could not find any, they came back home.
And, when they got back, they all stayed there.

Meanwhile, the two women were in the Meadows Above.
They married the Star Men and stayed there.

Then the younger one said to the other:
"Our mother, our father, our kinsmen must all feel bad
since they can't find any trace of us.

It was you, of course, who wanted so much to come here.
When you said so, I believed you,
and I have come with you so far as this.
We have made my father unhappy.
We have made my mother unhappy.
We have made my kinsmen unhappy.
It was all your idea!

"Our mother gave us very good advice.
but *you* didn't believe her!
When you had a bad dream,
then you didn't pierce your ears.
That's what you did, and now, here we are!
But I'm going back. If you want to stay here, stay here.
It makes me feel miserable to think of my parents.
I'm sorry to say these things, but I have said them.
When I think about it, I feel terrible."
It was the younger sister who was talking.

Then, her elder sister spoke:
"So then, let's both go back, some way or another.
But, in the meantime, let's go gather some kind of food.
Perhaps, in time, we can find a way to get back home."

So they stayed there
and each one of them had a child.
They went a little way off together,
and there they built a house,
and, when they had built it, they lived there.

And, after some time had passed,
they said: "These children of ours want some sinew."

So, their two husbands gave them sinew.

And then, again, later, the women said: "They want sinew."

The husbands gave it.

The women rolled the sinew on their thighs.
Every day, they said: "The children want sinew."
And their husbands gave it to them.

And those two women kept rolling it on their thighs,
and, when it was dark, they made a rope, those two.
And, letting it down toward the earth,
they took its measure.
"It might be hanging down just far enough!" they said.

But it didn't hang very far down,
so still the women said to their husbands:
"The children want sinew!
These children eat a lot, and nothing but sinew!"

And their husbands believed them.
The two women kept making rope until they had enough.
It reached all the way down,
all the way down to the ground below.

And then those two, leaving their children behind,
tied the rope and came down,
and, when they were halfway down,
the children began to cry.
They cried and cried.

Then, one of the Star Men said:
"What's the matter with those children?
Perhaps you'd better go see."

So, the other one went to the women's house,
but when he got there,
no one was there except the children, crying.
He looked all around,
and there was the rope, hanging straight down.
Then he cut it,
and the two women, who had almost reached the ground,
fell and died.

One of their brothers, who was still hunting for them,
saw them. The rope was also there.
He took it back home and told the others:
"These sisters of ours, these two women, are dead."

Then the kinsmen went,
and, when they got to where the women lay,
they lifted them up and carried them home.
And, when they had carried them there,
they laid them down in the water.
Then, in the morning, the two women awoke,
and they came up out of the water and went home.

After awhile, the younger sister spoke.
"My sister spoke to me first,
and then, we talked together
about how we looked with great wonder
at those Star Men. I went along with her.
During the dancing time, we dreamed of those Star Men,
but there seemed to be no way for us to get to them.
We talked so much,
talking of everything with delight!
That's what we did, talking together.
And then, our Star Men brought us to themselves
and made love to us, and we all played together.
But when we set out to return home,
they found out about it
and cut the rope as we were climbing down,
and so, we died."
That's what the younger sister said.

The two sisters told their mother all about it.
The younger sister said:
"One of the Star Men looked very red,
and he ate only hearts!
Another looked bluish,
and *he* ate only fat!
There seem to be a lot of Star Beings,

each one eating just one kind of a thing or another.
Some eat just liver, some eat just flesh.
That's the way the Star Beings are!"

The elder sister said nothing, then.

And then, long ago, they all stayed there together.

That's all of it, they say.

The Moon and Frog Old Woman

Once, long ago,
the Moon was a little way beyond Hanýlekim Valley, they say.
From there,
he wandered to somewhere in the North Country.
He built a house and lived there.

From there, he went stealing.
He stole children, they say,
and took them home with him.

Now, Moon was living with his sister.
Their house was coated with ice.
So, when he had brought the stolen children together,
no one could do anything about it.
They couldn't crawl into his house
because, as soon as they tried to scramble up to the
        smokehole,
they slid down—they couldn't get up to it!
There was nothing they could do about it.

Moon became arrogant
because they couldn't get at him.
Even though they followed him home from all the country
        'round,
they couldn't kill him.

By and by,
he went off to the North Country thieving again.
And he kept going,
searching, searching through all the houses roundabout.

Then, he came to where Frog Old Woman was living,
in a winter house.

And that old woman was weaving a big burden basket.
She held the bunch grass in her mouth without dropping it.

As she was weaving, Moon came along,
and he sat down by the fire, and stayed there for a while.
Finally, she said: "How is everything with you?"
It was the old woman who said it.

"Oh, all right, just like always," he said.
"I'm weary, travelling about. I get lonesome."

Just then,
the old woman's grandchild came out of the house to play.
Then, Moon crawled out and grabbed the child.
He stole him and made off with him.

Meanwhile, the old woman kept weaving, just weaving.
And, as she wove, she thought:
"I wonder why that child isn't making any noise."
So then, she put down her weaving and crawled outside.
But the child was nowhere to be seen.

She followed the child's footprints,
but, when she got to where the child had been playing,
Moon had already grabbed him and carried him away.

Furiously, that old woman set out in pursuit.
She went in pursuit.

Now, when Moon had run a little way along,
by magic, he thought into being a stand of willows—
a stand of willows, wonderful to see.
And then again, when he had come along a little further,
he thought another stand of willows into being.
And then he hastened on.

The old woman, coming along behind,
ran up to the stand of willows,
still holding bunchgrass in her mouth.
When she saw the willows, she said:

"Well!
I have never seen anything so big and wonderful!"
And she stopped in her tracks and gathered some.
For a while, she went around breaking them off, one by one.

Then she remembered the child.
And when she remembered him, she sprang up quickly.
She ran on a little ways.
There was another stand of willows, lovely to see.
She ran to where they were, stopped and gathered some.
She went around, breaking off branches, one by one.

Just at that moment, she called her child to mind;
so off she went, running after Moon.

Just as she almost caught up with him,
he got home.
He had planned to escape
while she looked with wonder on the stands of willows
and while she stopped to gather some of them.
And he did escape,
but she almost caught up with him.

When he had crawled up on his earth lodge,
he sent the child inside,
and flopped himself down by the smokehole.

The old woman crawled up and up the side of the house,
but, when she got a little ways up,
she slipped down again.
And she crawled up again,
but, when she got nearly halfway up,
she slid down as before.

She stood up.
"Whatever it takes, I'll crawl to where you are!" she said.
And she crawled up again.
She kept crawling up and crawling up,
but, halfway to the smokehole, she slipped,
and she slid, little by little, back down to the ground.

"Curses!" she said.
"I *will* crawl up to you!"

She got to her feet and started up again.
Though she came close to losing her balance,
time and time again,
she got to the top at last!

Then Frog Old Woman spoke.
"Get out of my way!" she said.
"I'm crawling in! Get out of my way!"

But Moon did not answer.

"Do you hear?" she asked.
"Make room for me, quickly! I'm crawling in!
I've come after that grandson of mine!
How did you come to bring him here?
Did you think I gave him to you,
or did you just steal him from me?
Get out of my way! I'm crawling in!
Get out of my way!
If you *don't* get out of my way,
I'm going to swallow you!
Do you hear?
I'm telling you to get out of the way, right now!
Step aside!
If you *don't,* I'm going to swallow you!"

Then, Moon answered her and said:
"If you want to swallow me, then swallow me.
Do what you want to do."

"Just be quiet!
Be quiet if you don't want me to swallow you!"

"Go ahead! Swallow me if you want to," said Moon,
still flopped down by the smokehole.

The old woman grabbed him and held him.
"Now, I've got you," she said,
and she swallowed him.
And, when she had swallowed him,
she sat there and blinked her eyes several times,
and then she gagged.
She kept gagging because she had swallowed the Moon.

And he kept growing and growing in her stomach
until he grew a little way out of her mouth.

She gagged.

And, as he kept growing, that old woman died.
Her belly filled till it burst.
She burst apart, and he killed her.

Then Moon spoke.
"You're a bad frog who won't chase anybody any more.
You'll stay along the rivers and not do anything to anyone!
And, from now on,
since you go around swallowing people,
you'll have a big mouth."

And he himself was the one
that Frog Old Woman was going to swallow,
time and time again.
Every time, he was shoved partly in,
little by little,
one side going in until it disappeared;
then, little by little, he grew,
and, when he seemed full-grown,
he gazed upon himself.
From olden times,
he is the one who is swallowed, again and again.

Now, later, after he had killed Frog Old Woman,
and he and his sister had been living there a while,
he spoke to her.

"You'd better go out at night," he said.
"You'd better be the moon."

"All right," she said.

"I'm going to be the sun," he said.
And he started off.

Now, the woman went at night, they say,
but some Star Men waylaid her—
they were going to grab her and pull her down,
but she saw them, and they stopped where they were.
And there they are, those Star Men,
huddled together in the very place where they have stood
      since long ago,
ashamed of having pursued that woman.

Then the sister said to her brother:
"*You'd* better go at night.
Those Star Men intend to waylay me when they pursue me,
but they are ashamed when I see them coming,
and they don't grab me.
Men who do things like that bother me a lot."

"Indeed so," said her brother.
"Let *me* be the Moon,
and *you* be the Sun Woman!
And people will be told:
'That's what they did in the old days,
and Frog Old Woman is still swallowing the Moon.'
And everyone will look at me," he said.
"And people will look, too, at those who pursued my sister—
those who became ashamed,
stopped, and are standing there still.
They stand there because they pursued her
and were ashamed.
That's what people will talk about when they tell old tales."

And then, they set out,
and Moon Man, floating up,

met Sun Woman, floating down,
and asked: "How are you?"

The woman answered: "Nothing is disturbing me."

"That is well," said Moon.
"Let it be so forever."

That's all of it.

Old Man Thunder and the Theft of Fire

It seems that there were once some people
who lived crowded together in a great sweatlodge.
Some went hunting around there,
but one of them who went did not come back.

Darkness came, and then, the dawn.
Again the darkness came and again the dawn.

Then, one of them spoke.
"Why doesn't one of you go look for him?" he said.

Then, in the morning, a man went,
but *that* one who went did not return either.

Dawn came, and, in the morning,
another man set out
and made his way down along the ridge.

Then a stranger appeared,
and, when they met, he spoke.
"We two will wrestle with each other," he said.

But the other man said,
"I'm not going around looking for anything like that.
I'm just out hunting deer."

"But I *am* going to grab you and wrestle with you,"
said the stranger.

They wrestled with each other
and the stranger killed that man.
Great Green Lizard did that terrible thing!

When darkness fell, the man had not come back.
And so, again, the next morning,
someone set out to search for him.
This third man travelled down along the same ridge
until he came to the wrestling place.
When he looked around,
he saw fir needles scattered around,
his kinsman cut to pieces,
and the skin stretched out on the ground.

Just then, Great Green Lizard came up to him and said,
"What are you doing, wandering around?
Did you come here to wrestle?"

"Well," said the man,
"though I didn't come here wanting to wrestle,
if that's what you want to do,
then let's the two of us wrestle!"

They wrestled. The Great Green Lizard killed that man.

It got dark,
and the last man who had gone searching did not come back.
Dawn came,
and in the morning a fourth man set out.
He went along more or less as the others had gone
until he came to the wrestling place.

And, again, Great Green Lizard came up and said,
"What are you doing here?"

"What do you *think* I'm doing?" said the man.
"I'm just travelling around, that's all."

"Well, now," said Great Green Lizard,
"you don't seem like someone who just goes around for no
        reason.
Let's wrestle!"

The two of them wrestled,
and, again, Great Green Lizard killed his man.
And, when he had nicely skinned and cut him up,
Great Green Lizard carried him away.
He took only the meat away, and left the bones.
There those bones were, lying scattered around, horrible to
    see.

Again, it was that, as darkness came,
the man did not return.
And, by and by, people were talking.
They said, "What in the world could have happened?"

"I, myself, will go and see," said the leader.
"Stay here, everybody, and don't go wandering around.
We are in an evil and mysterious country."

He spoke to his two children—his daughter and son.
"You two stay safely here with everyone.
Don't go wandering off! Stay here!
Whatever country this is,
it is certainly strange and frightening.
Perhaps I shall not return again," he said.
The two of you just stay here, out of danger.
My daughter, if I don't return, look after your younger brother."

"Very well," she said.

He went, and, as with the others,
when darkness came, he did not return.

"Our father must also have died," said the sister.
"He said it would be so, if he did not return."

They went to sleep, and when day broke, he had not come
    back.
Those two waited until dark, but he did not come back.

Sometime later, the sister was pounding acorns.
And then she sent her little brother for wood.

"You'd better gather some wood," she said.
"Don't go far! Pick up the wood that's near here,
and then you can come back with it," she said.

So then he went to gather wood,
but he brought back only pitchy stumps.

"I didn't ask for such big chunks as these," she said.
"Just bring some little sticks.
You might hurt yourself lugging in those big chunks!
But you must not go far off.
There are many magical and powerful beings in this country."

"What powerful beings are you talking about?" asked the boy.

"The ones that have done these things to us—
that have done our father and his kinsmen in,"
answered his sister.

The next day, at first light, she sent him again to get wood.
"You'd better get more wood.
When it gets dark, let's make a fire," she said.

And so, he went to gather some.
But he came back carrying huge pitchy chunks of wood.

"I didn't ask you to carry back such big pieces as that?"
said his sister.

They went to sleep, the boy and his sister,
and, in the morning, they awoke.

"I'm going out hunting," said the boy.

But his sister forbade him.
"That's not what I told you to do. I must keep you here,"
she said.

"You say that the country roundabout
is full of powerful and mysterious beings," said the boy.

"What can such creatures do to me?
I, too, am a powerful and dangerous being!
I'm going," he said.   And he went.

He travelled down along the ridge,
going on and on
until he came to the place where the others had been killed.
Their bones, scattered all around, were horrible to see.

The boy took a look around.
Just then, a being was coming toward him,
and, as he got closer, he said:
"What are you doing, wandering around here?"

"Oh, nothing in particular," said the boy.

"Would you like to wrestle?" asked the other.

"It's all right with me," the boy said.

So they wrestled, and the boy killed Great Green Lizard.
Then, he went home again and bathed in warm water.

He said to his sister: "You'd best stay here!
But I am going away!
On the trails through the Meadows Above,
that's where I shall be!
I shall set out from here,
and, when I arrive in the Meadows Above,
the world will rumble!"

"Very well," said his sister.

And he went, leaving his sister behind.
And just as he got there, the world rumbled.
It seemed as if the world resounded with a mighty rumbling!

In those old times, his sister stayed just where she was.

But the boy kept rumbling around in the Meadows Above.
He was a tiny creature—a little being with big eyes.
As he went, people could hear him from far away.
The rumbling came down somewhere in the south;
and then, from the north, from the land beyond,
it started up again.
And, as he circled over the middle of the world,
the thundering stopped.

And then, winter came to the land.
As winter set in, there was silence.
Thunder could not be heard.

But, when it got to be springtime,
people could hear him. He made a great noise.
In each and every place, he travelled over the land.
He made them hear him everywhere, circling above them.

Then it seemed to the people that he had gone away,
for, as autumn came, they couldn't hear him.
It was like that all through the winter.
But then, when spring came—his old rumbling time—
he rumbled!

He travelled all around through the Meadows Above,
going round and round about throughout the land,
but, when autumn came again, he stayed quiet.

Now, Mosquito was Thunder's cousin.
And the two of them stayed together in the Meadows Above.
All through the winter, they stayed together.

When spring came again, and Mosquito was about to leave,
they talked together.

"Where can we find something to kill and eat?" asked Thunder.

"I can manage to survive by just hunting anywhere,"
answered Mosquito.

"All right! I'll do that way too," said Thunder.
And then he thundered.
His children set out,
and with them seemed to come a great rain.
And when they came home again, and stayed there,
then the rain began to stop,
and all the leaves and grass burst forth.
It was beautiful to see!

Now, there were human beings living in a certain place,
and Mosquito flew down to suck their blood.
And, when his belly was full, he flew away.
He carried the blood back up with him,
and, when he had gotten home,
he made the blood into a little piece of meat.
Then he gave it to his children.
There was just enough for each one of them,
and there they stayed.
But there was only enough for one meal.

So, when morning came and everyone was awake,
Mosquito returned to the place where all the people were
    living.
And he flew down and sucked their blood.
And, when he had sucked their blood,
he set out for home again.
He kept going until he got there,
and, when he got there,
he made the blood into a thing just like a piece of meat,
and he roasted it for his children,
and, when it was cooked, he gave it to them to eat.

Then, Thunder asked: "Where did you get that?
Though I have hunted all over everywhere,
I haven't yet killed anything at all."
That's what Thunder said to Mosquito.

But Mosquito said nothing.
He just stayed there and said nothing.
He was very frightened.

"If I should tell him how I get food,
something bad will happen,
so I'll just keep quiet about it!" he thought.
It was Mosquito talking to himself.
Without saying anything, he just went away.

In the morning, he kept going along
until he arrived in this country, far from the Meadows Above.
Mosquito came to this land to go hunting here and there.

Meantime, Thunder kept roaming around there,
up there, in the Meadows Above.
There he was, wandering around, hunting for something.

Now, Mosquito, flying around from one place to another,
was sucking blood.
And, when he had sucked enough, he set out for home.
He travelled home from the hunt until he got there,
and, when he got there, he stayed there.
After that, he roasted the food
and gave his children their evening meal.

By and by, Thunder spoke.
"You seem to have come from a wonderful country—
a great country to hunt in," he said.
"Why don't we all move?
Let's cross over to West Mountain and live there!
From there, you know, I can get to every place in the world!"

So, from somewhere to the south,
they all moved across to West Mountain and built a house.
It was a big sweatlodge, and they all lived there.

From there, Mosquito went to hunt again.
He went along until he got down below,
and then he searched all around
until he found a place where some people were living.
When he had gotten there and sucked their blood,
he carried it off back home again.

Meanwhile, Thunder had come home from hunting, too.

When they had both come back, they talked together.

"Where did you get the blood?" asked Thunder.

Mosquito didn't answer.

Since autumn was coming, Thunder said:
"Let's stay here through the winter."

"Very well," said Mosquito.
"When springtime comes,
we can kill all kinds of things to eat."

And so, they stayed through the winter.
It was freezing weather, and they were all very cold.

Thunder spoke.
"This winter time is no good!" he said.
"It's terrible! When winter comes and everything freezes,
it's just no good!
Can you see anything for us to kill?"
He was talking to Mosquito.
Thunder was asking Mosquito.

"Maybe so and maybe not," answered Mosquito.
And he thought to himself:
"I mustn't tell him much of anything
because he sounds like a really terrible creature.
If I let him know where the people are,
he'll probably do them in!
So, I'll keep it a secret.
It will be good if I don't say anything.
Now, if I just go from here to someplace else
and suck a little blood from people,
then I'll stay alive.
But, if I talk to this Thunder fellow
and tell him that I suck blood from human beings,
then he will go out after them

and kill all the people.
Then I would starve!"
That is what Mosquito thought,
so he didn't tell Thunder anything.

Then they stayed there together
until it was almost springtime.

Old Man Thunder spoke.
"Though the weather's still cold,
it's almost spring," he said, talking to Mosquito.
"It seems to me there should be some people living around
    here.
Have you seen any?"

But Mosquito said: "No. I haven't seen a single one!"

"Well, now," said Thunder,
"Since the winter is so cold in this country around here,
there must be people who make fires.
So, what I say is that if we steal their fire,
then we can stay warm in the wintertime."
It was Thunder who spoke, putting his plan to Mosquito.

But then Mosquito said: "It's wicked of you to talk that way!
You mustn't think of killing people! You must be good!"
And then Mosquito sat there and said nothing more.

Springtime came, and Thunder went hunting.
He killed and ate anything he could find.

Mosquito went hunting, too.

Then Thunder thundered and rumbled.
There was a mighty banging and crashing in the world,
terrible to hear.

So, they both travelled around,
and, just at dusk, they came home from hunting.
Mosquito brought back his little piece of meat.

But Thunder,
who had been going around and about over the countryside,
came home just as it was getting dark, and said:
"I see that there are people like me who have fire.
Now, if we steal it, then, when winter comes again,
we two won't be so miserable."
That's what Thunder said. He wanted to steal the fire.

But Mosquito said: "What you say is bad!
Don't bother them! Leave them alone!
You are not going to make human beings miserable!"

But Thunder wouldn't agree with that.
"Do you want to be the one who is miserable,
freezing through another winter?" he asked.
"I'm just not willing to suffer like that.
I'm stealing it, I'm going to steal it!" said Thunder.

Mosquito angrily disagreed with him.
He thought it over for a little while; then he said:
"If you can't agree with me about this,
then you are a terrifying and evil being!
There, where people are,
is where my children and I will survive.
Since I can't look at things the way you do,
I'm going away."
It was Mosquito who spoke.

And at dawn, he went off hunting.
When he had gone along for a while, he saw some people.
He sucked their blood and carried it home
and roasted it and gave it to his children.

But Thunder came back there too, and he asked:
"Where did you get that food?"

Mosquito answered.
"I'm going to tell you," he said.
"If you'll promise not to kill too many of them,
I'll tell you."

"All right," said Thunder,
"I won't kill too many. I'll kill just enough to get by."

"I'll tell you tomorrow," said Mosquito.

After they had slept, when the sun came up,
and it was morning, they set out to go hunting again.
Now, Mosquito sent Thunder off in some other direction
from the one he, himself, took.

He went to his usual place,
and, when he had gotten there,
and had sucked out the blood from the people,
he took it home again.
It was a little piece of meat that he carried.
After he had been home awhile,
he roasted the meat and gave it to his children.

But then, later, he spoke to Thunder.
"I got this meat by killing a tree," he said.
"One of those standing trees that are full of pitch.
I don't kill very many of them.
But that's what I did. I brought it home and ate it.
Perhaps you'll try that yourself!"

"All right," said Thunder.

"You are—you mustn't disturb those people too much,"
    said Mosquito.
"You ought not to kill a lot of them.
It will be enough for you to kill just one."

Then, "All right," said Thunder.

Again at dawn, Mosquito set out.
When he had gotten to his usual place,
and had sucked blood, he started home from hunting.

Meanwhile, there was a great noise,
and the earth rumbled with a mighty echoing roar,

and it seemed as if the ground shook all over the world.

Mosquito heard this as he was going along.
He got back home, and, after he was there,
Thunder arrived.

"I got one!" he said. It was Thunder who spoke.

"Well, now," said Mosquito, "I want to talk to you!
You must not bother people! Leave them alone!
I'm going away now. I shall be Mosquito.
When it gets on toward wintertime,
When autumn comes, then I'll disappear.
But then, when it's springtime,
I'll be born again.
When the ground is wet, there will be many of me!
I will not really be gone,
for when I will seem to have just disappeared,
I will survive!
By sucking the blood of people,
I will survive!
When I talk about people,
I really mean those tree people.
That's just the way I talk.
And you must just kill one of them at a time,
not lots of them."

"Very well," said Thunder, "I won't kill them in bunches."

So then, next day, they went hunting.

Thunder struck a tree, and he said:
"That's just the way my killing is going to be done!
It's no good for trees to be standing around a long time!"

After that, he set out for somewhere around here,
and, when he got there,
he saw a house where some people were living,
and he stole their fire, and carried it away.
Again, he flung a bolt, striking a tree,

and the tree blazed up and burned
when Thunder struck it with fire.
He was very powerful.

Later, when he had returned, he said:
"I have stolen fire from some people.
Then I struck another tree.
When I did it, when I struck it with fire, it was *good*!"

Then Mosquito was angry,
but Thunder said: "It's all right! It was *good*!"

"But about the fire," said Mosquito,
"when I told you not to do a thing like that,
I spoke well and wisely."

"You're right," said Thunder.
"Next time, I'll go with you to get food."

Then they slept,
and, in the morning, Thunder went away,
but Mosquito stayed in the lodge.
When Thunder had been gone for a while,
then Mosquito gathered up his things and left.
He said to himself:
" 'In olden times, long ago, Mosquito was angry with his
        cousin,
and, since he was angry, he went away from everyone.'
That's what people will say about me
when they're telling old tales.
'He was angry and he went away from everyone.' "
That's what Mosquito said to himself.
And he came out of the sweatlodge and went away.

He came this way, looking for a home.
"I wonder where I can stay and manage to survive," he said.
"Perhaps I *do* know the kind of place where I can survive.
And *then* I will be Mosquito!"

So he made his home under the bushes,
and there, under the bushes,
mosquitoes have lived ever since.

Meanwhile, Thunder came back to the empty lodge,
back to the place on West Mountain
from which his cousin had angrily departed.
"Just because I didn't pay any attention to what he told me,
my cousin is angry," said Thunder.
"But nevertheless, I am not going to stop doing what I do!"

Then, at dusk, he went to sleep.
And, as day broke over the land,
he set out, they say, going to steal fire.
And, going, he came to a land where people lived,
and stole their fire.

Now, the rain bore him, going.

He looked over the land,
and he saw the smoke of many fires drifting up.
Then, seeking them out, he stole them,
and he kept on stealing them
until he had stolen them from each and every place
where people lived.
Then, he carried them to his lodge,
and when he had carried them there, he stayed.
He stayed, being very warm, they say.
His house was wonderfully warm, they say.

By and by, he searched for someone to hire.
He asked, and, when he asked,
Nighthawk said: "I am one who will not go to sleep!
i'm not one who goes to sleep!"
It was Nighthawk who said it,
whereupon, Old Man Thunder paid him with a necklace.
He benecklaced him, and they stayed there.
And, standing guard at the smokehole of the sweatlodge,
Nighthawk talked on and on.

But after that, there was no fire in any place,
and the people couldn't make fire.

So the elders hired this Magpie.
When they had shot deer and gotten the meat ready—
when they had spread it down,
then Magpie stared at it.
As he kept staring at it,
it got just singed enough to turn gray on top.

"There you are!" said Magpie.

And the elders ate it,
and, after them, all the people did, indeed, eat underdone
        meat!

Coyote spoke.
"Since I am, without doubt, an important man,
you must all make Magpie do that for me."

But his brother-in-law spoke.
"You mustn't say a thing like that!" he said.
"When you talk like that, it sounds terrible!
You say bad things!"

Later, the people looked out over the countryside,
hoping to see smoke from a fire.
They did not see any.
The next day, they looked again,
but they did not see any.

Meanwhile, two Lizard brothers were lying together,
close by the earth lodge,
and, along toward morning, they spoke:
"Look, there is smoke on West Mountain!"

Coyote scooped up some dirt and threw it in their eyes.
"West Mountain indeed!
Those two don't know *what* they're seeing.

That's the way they *always* see,
with little eyes like theirs!"

Then, Coyote's brother-in-law spoke angrily to him.
"That's the way you always act!
Why are you always bad that way?"

Disgusted, Coyote spoke.
"Those two boys saw nothing at all.
They lie when they speak," he said.

But then, the village leader crawled out of the smokehole.
He said: "Do you see it, you two?"

And the brothers said: "Look, there is smoke on West Mountain!"

Everyone looked across,
and, when they looked, the smoke was on West Mountain,
like a tiny tree, standing there.

And, when they had seen it, they sent one all around.
He went all around,
all around to every place.

Then the people came.
They kept coming.
They came together.
And, when they were all together,
their leaders spoke to them.

"Muster your spiritual power!
Muster your power and send it out, all of you!" they said.

From each and every country,
they sent one person.
Only the frightening ones were chosen out,
only the sinuous ones.

Then, one by one, the people crawled into the lodge.
They tried to be quiet, but everyone could be heard.

Everyone made noise.

At last, Mouse tried.
He crawled in, and crawled around inside,
and they couldn't hear him.

Then the leaders spoke.
"He's the one!" they said.

At dawn, they started off.
All kinds of creatures went.

Deer went. Jackrabbit went. Dog went.
Mouse went. Fisher went.
All kinds of creatures went.

Snake went.
Skunk went. He took his flute.

And so, they set out.
They kept going and going until they were halfway there.
They went a little further,
and, when they had almost arrived,
they squatted down and sat there.

While they were sitting there,
it got dark.
They all huddled together and sat there.

As it got dark, Nighthawk started babbling.
He babbled.
"One who doesn't sleep am I!" he said.
"Nighthawk am I!" he said.

"Woswoswoswoswoswos!
One who does not fail to see am I!
One who sees everything am I!" he said.

Meanwhile, they sent Mouse. He took Skunk's flute.

"Go!" said one of the leaders.
"They seem to have gone to sleep."

Then Mouse went.
He went on tiptoe.
He tiptoed from place to place until he got there.
When he had gotten there and tiptoed up,
he took a peek at Nighthawk's eyes.
Though his eyes were shut tight, he was speaking.
Nighthawk, bedecked with a necklace,
sat there and kept on speaking,
babbling on and on.

Then, Mouse gnawed through the necklace and stole it.

And Nighthawk was babbling.
"A creature who doesn't sleep am I!
Nighthawk am I!" he said.

And, when Mouse had stolen the necklace,
he crawled into the sweatlodge.
He crawled in, and down from the smokehole.

They were sleeping.
Snoring, they made a great racket.

When he had crawled around inside,
Mouse gnawed the skirts off Old Man Thunder's daughters.
He gnawed them through.
Then he stuck a burning ember into the flute,
and he put it on his back,
and he crawled out.

He carried it on his back,
and he ran to where all the people were.
Then he hastened away, carrying it on his back,
and Deer hastened away, taking some of the ember on his leg,
and Dog hastened away, sticking some under his ear.
They all ran back homewards, carrying the fire.

When they had gotten a little way off,
Old Man Thunder woke up,
and he and his daughters made a great rumble.
Old Man Thunder sprang to his feet,
and his daughters jumped up quickly.
But, as they started up,
their bark skirts fell off,
and they squatted down again,
and put their skirts in order.
Then they sprang up again,
and started in pursuit.

It was as if the earth was mightily rumbling and grumbling!
It was as if a great, great cloudburst
swept down upon the people.

Now, Deer threw the fire he was carrying at a cedar tree.
A little further on, Dog threw his fire at an elderberry tree.
Still further on,
when the women had almost caught up with them,
Mouse threw some of the fire in his flute at a buckeye tree.

And then, they ran homewards,
and Mouse was carrying just that fire in the flute
which he had saved back.

But the daughters overtook them,
and put out the fire.

There was water, and water was doused on the fire.
A cloudburst overtook them.

All that time, Skunk was spraying the daughters,
and Snake ran after them as if he was going to bite them.
The women gave up the chase,
and turned around and went back home.
Then, the skies cleared,
and everything was wonderful.

But the creatures *did* come back empty-handed.
When they got back, they said:
"They put the fire out on us!"

"I threw my fire into that bush there."
It was Dog who spoke.

"I threw mine into a cedar tree," said Deer.

"What I had in the flute,
I threw into a buckeye tree," said Mouse.
"From now on, we'll make fire with those."

Meanwhile, when Old Man Thunder got back to his own place,
he spoke.

"In this world,
I shall no longer be one who chases people around.
I shall be one whom human beings never see.
For, if I should stay in this world,
people would run after me and annoy me, I think.
So, I will go up from this land into the Meadows Above,
and when I have carried the fire there which I have stolen,
there will be no fire in this land."

So Old Man Thunder stole the fire,
and carried it to the Meadows Above.
He did a wicked thing about the fire!
He spoke:
"Now, I think I'll stay here,
wandering around in the meadows above,
having nothing to do with people.
I will be a rumbler sometimes, as I travel about.
And he stayed there.

After he was gone,
people made fire by gathering elderwood,
chopping it up and bringing it back.
And they hunted for cedarwood, and brought it back,
And they hunted for buckeye wood, and brought it back.

And, when they got home,
they made fire-drills from the cedar and buckeye,
and made fire.

And they said to each other:
"When people talk of these times, they'll say:
'Those creatures of ancient times
threw away what fire they had.
That way, they got fire.
When fire was stolen, they got it back.'
That's what people will say."

And there they were, long ago.
And that's the end of it.

Appendix

How This Translation Was Made

Dixon's recordings of Hánc'ibyjim's Maidu myths were published in 1912 as Volume IV of the *Publications of the American Ethnological Society,* edited by Franz Boas. The first 27 pages of the Creation Myth provide the Maidu text with an interlinear translation; the rest of the book (241 pages) has the Maidu and English versions on facing pages.

My task was to rectify and reconstitute Dixon's Maidu transcription, thereby restoring, as precisely as possible, exactly what Hánc'ibyjim said. Next, it was necessary to break down the reconstituted text into its minimal meaningful units and to establish a literal translation for each of these. Only when the complete meaning of the original Maidu was clear to me did I attempt to come up with an artful English version of the text—one which would be as close as possible to the meaning of the Maidu but which, at the same time, would delight and satisfy an English ear. Just as with the Maidu, the English should be most effective when heard, not read silently. Thus the best analog in our English tradition is the theater— drama—and, to a lesser extent, poetry—not written prose. That this is so is underscored by the prevalence of direct quotations and, often, quotations within quotations. Though we have little information on Hánc'ibyjim's style aside from the fact that he was described by people 50 years later as "the last great Maidu storyteller," we know that the tales were commonly told by assuming different voices for different characters, thus further enhancing the theatrical effect of the performance.

In order to exemplify the reconstitution process, I will take the first five sentences of the Creation Myth, showing Dixon's original transcription with my reconstitution in tandem just below. These clearly demonstrate the remarkably good quality of Dixon's transcription, considering the time and place in which the material was written down.

Ko'doyapem kan uniñ ko'do momim' opitmöni
k'ódojapem k'an, 'uním k'ódo momím 'opítmyni,

hintsetoyetsoiam. Hin'tsetoyewe'bisim homon'kodoi'dimaat
hínc'etojec'oj'am. hínc'etojewebisim, homóm k'ódojdi ma'át

nu'ktim kawim'maat tsemen'tsoia. Tsai'tsainom mai'düm
núktim k'awí ma'át c'eménc'oj'am. c'ájc'ajnom májdym

hesi'kimaat hesi'mmaat kai'noyementsoia. Amön'ikan
hesík'i ma'at, hesím ma'át kájnojemenc'oj'am. 'amýni k'an,

uniñ' kâ'dom tsewu'suktipem kâ'dom yotson'otsoia.
'uním k'ódom, c'ewúsuktipem k'ódo jýc'onoc'oj'am.

Epin'iñkoyo'di ko'do tsehe'hetsonopem yak'huböktsoia.
'epínim kojódi k'ódom c'ehéjhejc'onopem jákhybykc'oj'am.

My next step was to break down the reconstituted text into its smallest meaningful parts with a literal translation for each of these.

k'ódo – ja – pe – m k'an, 'uní –m
earth, land make [adjective [subject and, this [attributive
  forming case suffix]
  suffix] suffix]

k'ódo mom – ím 'opít – myni,
earth water [subject fill when,
[object case]
case]

hín – c'e – toje – c'oj – 'a – m.
float see all around it is [past [third person]
  said tense]

hínc'etoje – webis – im, homó – m
float, looking keep on [subject some [attributive]
around doing case] certain

k'ódoj – di ma'át, núkti – m k'awí ma'át,
earth, [locative indeed, a little [attrib.] dirt indeed
place case] bit [object
  case]

c'e –	mén –	c'oj'am.	c'ájc'ajno –	m	májdy –	m
see	not	(see above)	different kinds of	[attrib.]	creature(s)	[subj.]

hesí –	k'i	ma'at,	hesí –	m	ma'at,
what	[possessive case]	indeed	what	[subj.]	indeed

káj –	no –	je –	men –	c'oj'am.
fly	along	hither	not	(see above)

'amýni	k'an,	'uní –	m	k'ódo
thereupon	and,	this	[attrib.]	earth,

c'e –	wúsuk –	ti –	pe –	m	k'ódo,
see	impossible	[causative suffix]	[adj. suffix]	[attrib.]	land,

jý –	c'o –	no –	c'oj'am.	'epín –	im	kojó –	di
go	up and	along	(see above)	above	[attrib.]	meadow	in

k'odo –	m,	c'e –	héjhej –	c'o –	no –	pe –	m
earth	[subj.]	see	along after	up and over	along	[adj. suffix]	[attrib.]

ják –	hybyk –	c'oj'am.
resemble	seem like	(see above)

Here is a literal translation of these five sentences, incorporating all the bits of meaning in the original:

> And earthmaking [being], when water filled this earth, floated, looking all around, it is said. Keeping floating, looking all around, he didn't see any dirt, not even a little bit, they say. Different kinds of creatures of what sort, what kind were not flying around. Then he went up and around over this earth, impossible-to-make-see earth, they say. It seemed to look like the earth in the meadows above, look-throughable, they say.

My next step in the process—the one which involves the reader's willingness to trust the translator—was to look beyond the surface differences between the Maidu and English syntactic and inflectional structures in order to find an idiomatic, literate and, one hopes, interesting way to say what the Maidu says. This requires all the artfulness and sensitivity—and knowledge—that one can muster, along with a reliable ethical commitment not to unduly distort or abandon the meaning of the Maidu original. For example, I decided to prune away most of the "they say" phrases which translate the verb suffix -*c'oj*-, an element which must *always* occur in sentences wherein the narrator is reporting something which he did not, himself, see happen. English has, of course, no equivalent of this, so that this obligatory -*c'oj*- is, in fact, untranslatable.

Here is my final decision on how to translate this passage:

And Earthmaker, they say,
when this world was covered with water,
floated and look about him.

As he floated and looked about,
he did not see anywhere, indeed,
even a tiny bit of land.

No various creatures of any kind—
none at all were flying about.

And thus he travelled over this world,
over the engulfed land.

It seemed transparent,
like the land in the Meadows of Heaven.